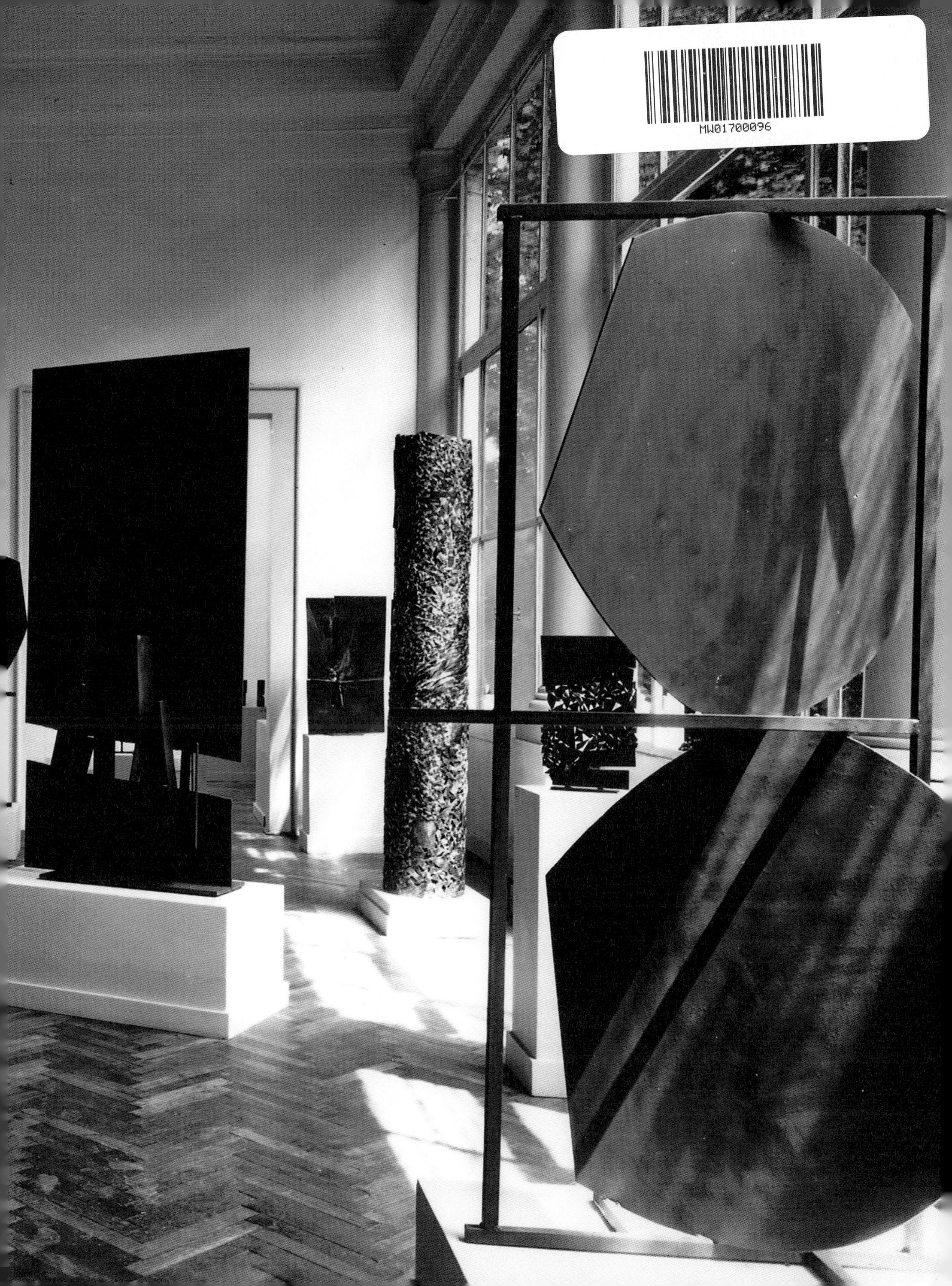

First published in 2017 by Osborne Samuel Ltd

www.osbornesamuel.com

ISBN: 978-1-9997293-1-8

Osborne Samuel would like to thank Stuart Hillcock of Footprint, who have designed and printed so many wonderful catalogues for us over many years.
Printed in the UK - www.fpiltd.com

Thanks also to Nick Moss from Todd White Photography for his excellent work

ASPECTS OF MODERN BRITISH SCULPTURE

The Post War Generation

September 27th – October 27th 2017

OSBORNE SAMUEL

MODERN AND CONTEMPORARY ART

23 Dering Street, London W1S 1AW
Tel: 020 7493 7939
www.osbornesamuel.com
info@osbornesamuel.com

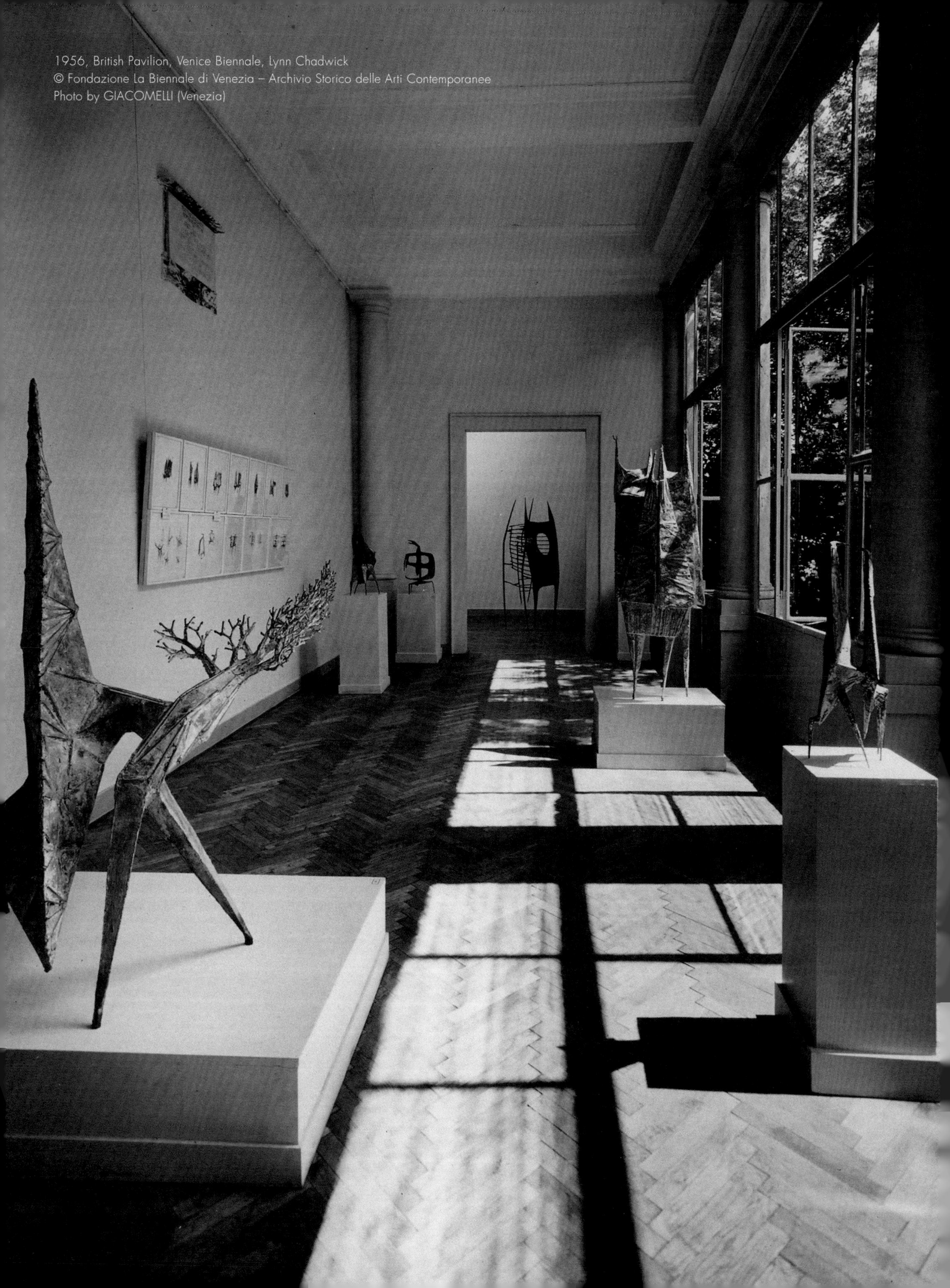

1956, British Pavilion, Venice Biennale, Lynn Chadwick
© Fondazione La Biennale di Venezia – Archivio Storico delle Arti Contemporanee
Photo by GIACOMELLI (Venezia)

Contents

Introduction

In 2005 Osborne Samuel commemorated the 1954 ground-breaking exhibition, Nine Abstract Artists, and republished Lawrence Alloway's influential book. The artists – Victor Pasmore, Kenneth & Mary Martin, Anthony Hill, Robert Adams, Adrian Heath, Terry Frost, Roger Hilton and William Scott - embracing formal abstraction, constructivism and a tachiste approach to painting, became synonymous with Alloway's book.

At the same time a group of sculptors, the core of this current exhibition, were championed internationally by the British Council throughout the 1950's. Robert Adams, Kenneth Armitage, Reg Butler, Lynn Chadwick, Geoffrey Clarke, Bernard Meadows, Eduardo Paolozzi, William Turnbull and Henry Moore were the artists selected for the British Pavilion in the 1952 Venice Biennale, entitled `New Aspects of British Sculpture.' Read wrote of the sculptors, "these new images belong to the iconography of despair, or of defiance and the more innocent the artist, the more effectively he transmits the collective guilt. Here are images of flight, of ragged claws `scuttling across silent seas,' of excoriated flesh, frustrated sex, the geometry of fear."

The term *Geometry of Fear* captured and continues to capture the imagination but it is not the full story of this defining moment in the history of British art. The term has become synonymous with the `spiky' metal forms of Meadows, Butler, Chadwick, Clarke, Armitage and Turnbull. There is no doubt that Meadows' crabs, threatening and scuttling, express much deeper emotions than simple anatomical representation. However, as Margaret Garlake candidly wrote, "the essential quality of the sculpture was produced and defined by the artist's adventurous and inventive attitude to materials and techniques." This includes Moore and Hepworth's carvings, stringed work, puncturing the solid form; it includes the work of Paolozzi studded with found objects and machine parts and it includes the carvings and constructions of Adams. Whether the materials were constructed, welded or carved, they were imbued with an energy beyond the physical form. Henry Moore wrote, "for me a work must first have a vitality of its own. I do not mean a reflection of the vitality of its own. I do not mean a reflection of the vitality of life, of movement, physical action, frisking, dancing figures and so on but that a work can have in it a pent-up energy, an intense life of its own, independent of the object it may represent. When a work has this powerful vitality we do not connect the word Beauty with it." [1]

This from the `father figure' of 20th century British sculpture who paved the way, gaining the International Sculpture Prize at the first Venice Biennale after the War in 1948. The British Council curated the British Pavilion at the Venice Biennales and Moore was later to acknowledge the role the Council played in launching his own career onto the international stage, alongside so many sculptors and artists of the post war generation.

Another important body, the Royal Society of Arts, was given the task of creating an event to commemorate the Great Exhibition of 1851 held at Crystal Palace. The centenary celebrations became the 1951 Festival of Britain. The remit of the Festival was `to display the British contribution to civilization, past, present and future, in the arts, in science and technology and industrial design.... The Festival must aim to bring into being new works of art ....And in many other ways leave behind

[1] Sculpture & Drawings, Vol 1 (1957) p.XXXi – taken from Hebert Read Modern Sculpture

some permanent contribution to the future. The Festival must be planned not merely as an end in itself but as an incentive to new effort and achievement. It must be used as a spring board."

There is no doubt that these aims were achieved but under a barrage of criticism in the austerity of post war Britain (although hopefully the organisers took comfort that the criticism was tame compared to the commentaries of the Great Exhibition of 1851. The Times writing for example "the finger of the Almighty would infallibly descend on such a presumptuous enterprise.") The Festival of Britain gave artists the opportunity to come to the foreground of British consciousness and many of these artists were then selected for exhibition at the British Pavilion in subsequent Venice Biennales and touring exhibitions organised by the British Council across Europe, North and South America. This assured their success abroad and later in their home country.

The 1952 British Pavilion at the Venice Biennale was a huge success judging both by the International press and the sales made. Chadwick's `Barley Fork' sold to Mr Alfred Barr, the first Director of the Museum of Modern Art, Peggy Guggenheim bought Armitage's 'People in Wind' from 1951 (version 3) and later bought Versions 1,2 and 4. Nelson Rockefeller subsequently also purchased many works from this group for his collection. Stuart Preston wrote in the New York Times July 1952 "The sculptors exemplify a ruthless reaction against the humanism of the remote past as well as a rejection of the hygienic intellectualism of the constructivists. Robert Adams, Reg Butler, Bernard Meadows and Eduardo Paolozzi are little known in America but will not remain so." This praise does not seem to have been shared by the British press as Alfred Barr felt the need to write to the Manchester Guardian in 1952, "Since the Bienniale Exposition of modern art at Venice will not close until mid-October it may not be too late to present some further opinion concerning the British participation. Arriving in England recently, I have come across your reviewer's account of the British Pavilion. As an American I can scarcely express my astonishment at her half-querulous, half-contemptuous critique of what seemed to many foreigners the most distinguished national showing in the whole Biennale..... Some of us thought this year that the British might have shot their bolt. We were wrong." Time has proved how right Alfred Barr was, as these artists continue to transfix collectors, museums, dealers and art historians alike.

For over 30 years Osborne Samuel have specialised in Modern British sculpture and been fortunate to have handled and exhibited many extraordinary sculptures from this pivotal era in the history of British art. We are extremely grateful to the Henry Moore Foundation and the Chadwick family who have for so many years supported our sculptural endeavours. This exhibition would also not have been possible without the very generous loans from collectors, friends of the gallery who share our passion for British sculpture - it would not be possible in a private gallery to have the breadth of sculpture under one roof without this support. I would like to thank Philip Wright for contributing excellent critical essays on the post war period and on each of our chosen artists. Lastly I would like to thank Peter Osborne and Gordon Samuel who have fired my own enthusiasm for this remarkable period in British art.

Tania Sutton

Henry Moore (1898-1986)

On refusing the offer of a knighthood in late 1950, Moore replied to the Prime Minister's office, 'I have been trying to consider how I myself should feel if I were addressed as 'Sir Henry' every day, even in my workshop, and I cannot help thinking that it would somehow change my conception of myself, and with it, the conception of my work .... I also feel that such a title might tend to cut me off from fellow artists whose work has aims similar to mine.' This response reflects the character of the miner's son from Yorkshire, an English county known for its pride not only in its landscape but also in its habit of plain speaking, in its occasional demonstrations of stubbornness, and in its down-to-earth approach to life. Rather than going into teaching as several of his siblings had done, given their father's ambition for his children to have a better life than working down a mine, this son had decided after his war service on the Western Front to become an artist.

The offer of a knighthood followed on the level of interest, recognition and esteem that Moore had visibly won internationally after 1945. He had had retrospectives in his native land (mi paese, as the Italians would say) at Leeds in 1941 and at Wakefield in 1944, acknowledging the contribution he had already made as an Official War Artist. International recognition came in the form of a retrospective at New York's Museum of Modern Art in 1946, and the award of the International Prize for Sculpture at the first post-war, rehabilitated-after-Fascism Venice Biennale in 1948. Both of these international events preceded a national 'crowning', with his nomination as the artist who would have the retrospective at the Tate Gallery to coincide with the Festival of Britain in 1951.

Promotion of his work by the British Council (at Venice) and the Arts Council (at the Tate) was astutely perpetuated by his participation in subsequent circulating solo and group, national and international exhibitions for the next twenty years or so. Thus in the following decade he would be seen as the leading ambassador for British modernism in sculpture and a symbol of the renewal of British creativity after the war. He also appeared to be a suitable, albeit unrelated, father figure for the next generation of British sculptors to emerge on the national and international stages (who are discussed below), a few of whom he had already generously invited at one time or another to assist him in his studio. When approached, Moore would willingly collaborate with broadcasters and filmmakers to explain the inspiration and demonstrate the making and siting of his work. It was inevitable that eventually a new generation of sculptors would wish to distance themselves from the form and the direction of his work, just as he himself originally had done, from the superfluous virtuosity of the academic sculpture of his predecessors.

In his early work Moore had sought out sources of inspiration beyond the Western canon – in African, Oceanic and particularly in pre-Columbian Mexican sculpture – in his effort to 'remove the Greek spectacles from the modern sculptor'. Later, in collaboration with his friend, the poet, art historian, writer, critic and anarchist Herbert Read, he would elaborate his now famous 'five sculptor's aims', headlined as truth to material, full three-dimensional realization, observation of natural objects and – more subjectively to be judged, perhaps – vision and expression, and vitality of power and expression. In formulating these aims, he assumed a sculptor's understanding of the natural materials that he uses – stone, wood, clay – and how by their very consistency, each of these materials would affect the shape of the work, imagining for example 'what a reclining woman would look like if flesh and blood were translated into the stone before him – the stone which has its own principles of form and structure ..... Moore believed that 'sculpture therefore is not a reduplication of form and feature; it is rather the translation of meaning from one material to another...'

Moore was a practical Yorkshireman, however, so eschewing Read's aesthetic interpretation of the sculptor's role, later in his life Moore explained to the filmmaker Warren Forma that 'a sculptor has to be a practical person ... if you're going to shape a piece of stone into a sculpture you must handle a hammer and chisel: you must be able to do it without knocking your hand; you must be a workman; you must be someone with his feet on the ground. .... A sculptor is a person obsessed with the form and shape of things .... (that pebbles and rocks show nature's way of treating stone; rocks show stone torn and hacked by cataclysmic forces, or eroded and polished by wind and rain; bones combine great structural strength with extreme lightness, the result being a natural tenseness of form) .... I would like to think my sculpture is a force, is a strength, is a life, a vitality from inside it, so that you can have a sense that the form is pressing from inside trying to burst or trying to give off the strength from inside itself...'

Moore was not the first twentieth century sculptor to resurrect direct carving, nor was he the first to weather the withering criticism of the acolytes of the academy. He acknowledged the direct carving by Rodin and his assistants, by Gauguin on occasion, and particularly by Brancusi, Modigliani and Epstein, both for their inspiration and for their technique. With the exception of Rodin, all of these had drawn on archaic or so-called primitive sources of inspiration, and their works had demonstrated a proper respect for the nature of the materials they used. As is well known, Moore's chosen themes centred on the female figure, predominantly the reclining figure, less often on seated figures, but frequently in groups – mother and child, or family groups presented frontally. These themes had already been seen in his work in the 1920's, but the encounter with Surrealism around 1930, with the recently executed 'bone structure' drawings and paintings of Picasso (showing his response to Surrealism, to which he himself never fully subscribed), the suggestive biomorphic forms of Hans Arp, the sheer fecundity of Giacometti's surrealist work during that decade, as well as the stricter geometry of his new neighbour Ben Nicholson – all these influences invaded and partly occupied Moore's repertoire of forms in the 1930's.

Nevertheless, there is a wealth of sketches and drawings to attest that Moore continued variations on the standing and the reclining figure during that decade. Their realization as sculptures was interrupted, but also enriched, by his work as an Official War Artist in his Shelter and the Coal Face drawings, and further compounded by the wartime shortage of carving and casting materials. Only towards the end of the war did the drawings materialize in the form of numerous terracotta and a few bronze 'sketch models' for single figures and family groups such as the 'Three standing figures' 1945.

Henry Moore (1898-1986)

This sketch model would serve as the maquette for the over life-size stone sculpture unveiled in 1948 at the first of several open air sculpture exhibitions at Battersea Park and Holland Park in the 1950's. Moore's sculptures were also regularly shown at the open air sculpture exhibitions at Middelheim near Antwerp, in Amsterdam and some other European cities.

While the 'Three Standing Figures' were close to figurative representations arising out of the character of his family groups, Moore then turned to a more surrealist, quasi insect-like representation of the figure, as here in 1950, and another softer, almost hand-formed modulation in 1953. Such standing figures would eventually be built up into a significantly solid, over life-size group of 'Upright Forms' in 1955-56, recalling – scarcely accidentally – a crucifixion scene, whose organic forms towered over the landscape. Already before the war, Moore had begun to photograph not only his full-size sculptures but also his maquettes against the landscape, to illustrate the parallels he wished to draw to the organic forms of his reclining figures. Towards the end of the 1950's that parallel would increasingly be reversed, as his series of 'Two Piece Reclining Figures' appeared to represent rock formations in nature, which were seen to resemble the encrusted remains of human figures.

Not unlike the unexpected throwbacks in Picasso's oeuvre, two small works from 1953 shown here demonstrate minor variations in Moore's repertoire of forms. The startling surrealist maquette of 'Mother and Child' appears to depict not the expected tenderness and intimacy of the theme, but hostility and struggle between parent and offspring, both figures suggesting a mutant rather than a human origin reminiscent of Picasso's late-1920's aggressive figures. It is not known if this was created of the sculptor's own volition, or specifically for an exhibition entitled 'Violence in contemporary art' at which it was shown. The maquette for the 'Reclining Warrior' identifies him by his missing limbs, but he is bereft of the shield which Moore's 'Falling Warrior' holds up for protection. Although he made several works in the Warrior series, the subject of the male figure remains rare in his oeuvre as does the theme of pain, humiliation and mutilation.

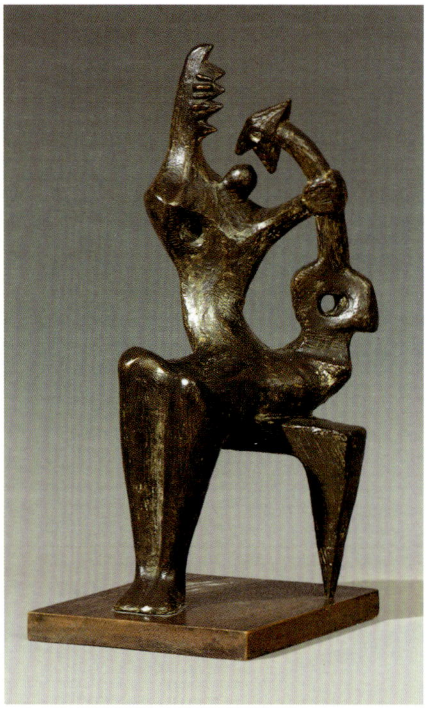

Right:
Mother & Child, 1953
Bronze with light brown patina
Height: 50.8 cm (20 in)
(Reference: LH2/315)

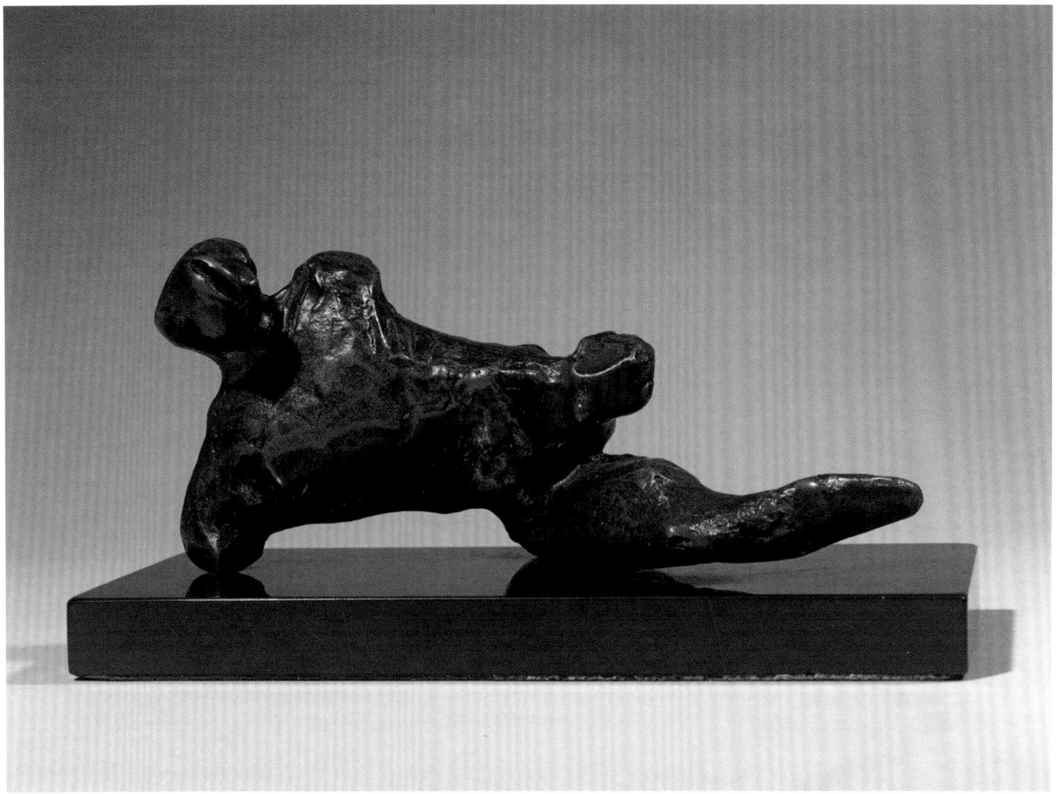

Reclining Warrior, 1953
Bronze
Edition of 9
8.5 x 19.7 x 9.5 cms (3¼ x 7¾ x 3¾ in)

Provenance
Private Collection, Canada

Literature
Alan Bowness, ed., *Henry Moore Complete Sculpture, 1949-1954,*
vol. 2, London, 1986, no. 358b, p. 53

Henry Moore (1898-1986)

Three Standing Figures, 1945
Bronze
Edition of 7, numbered on the top of the base.
Stamped with foundry mark 'C. VALSUANI CIRE PERDUE' (on the back of the base)
Conceived and cast in 1945
22.7 x 16.4 x 10.2 cms (9 x 6½ x 4 in)

Provenance
Buchholz Gallery (Curt Valentin), New York
Mrs. Nelson A. Rockefeller, New York, acquired from the above, November 1950
Christie's, New York, 7 November 2007, lot 513
Estate of Ronald P. Stanton, acquired from the above
Private Collection, UK

Literature
W. Grohmann, *The Art of Henry Moore,* New York, 1960 (monumental stone version illus. pls.129-132)
R. Melville, *Henry Moore, Sculpture and Drawings, 1921-1969,* London, 1970
(monumental stone version illus. figs.365-367)
D. Mitchinson, ed., *Henry Moore, Sculpture*, London, 1981, p.311, no.190
(plaster version illus. p.100; monumental stone version illus. p.101)
D. Sylvester, ed., *Henry Moore, Complete Sculpture, 1921-1948*, London, 1988, vol.1, p.16 no.258
(terracotta version illus. p.164; monumental stone version illus. pp.165-168)

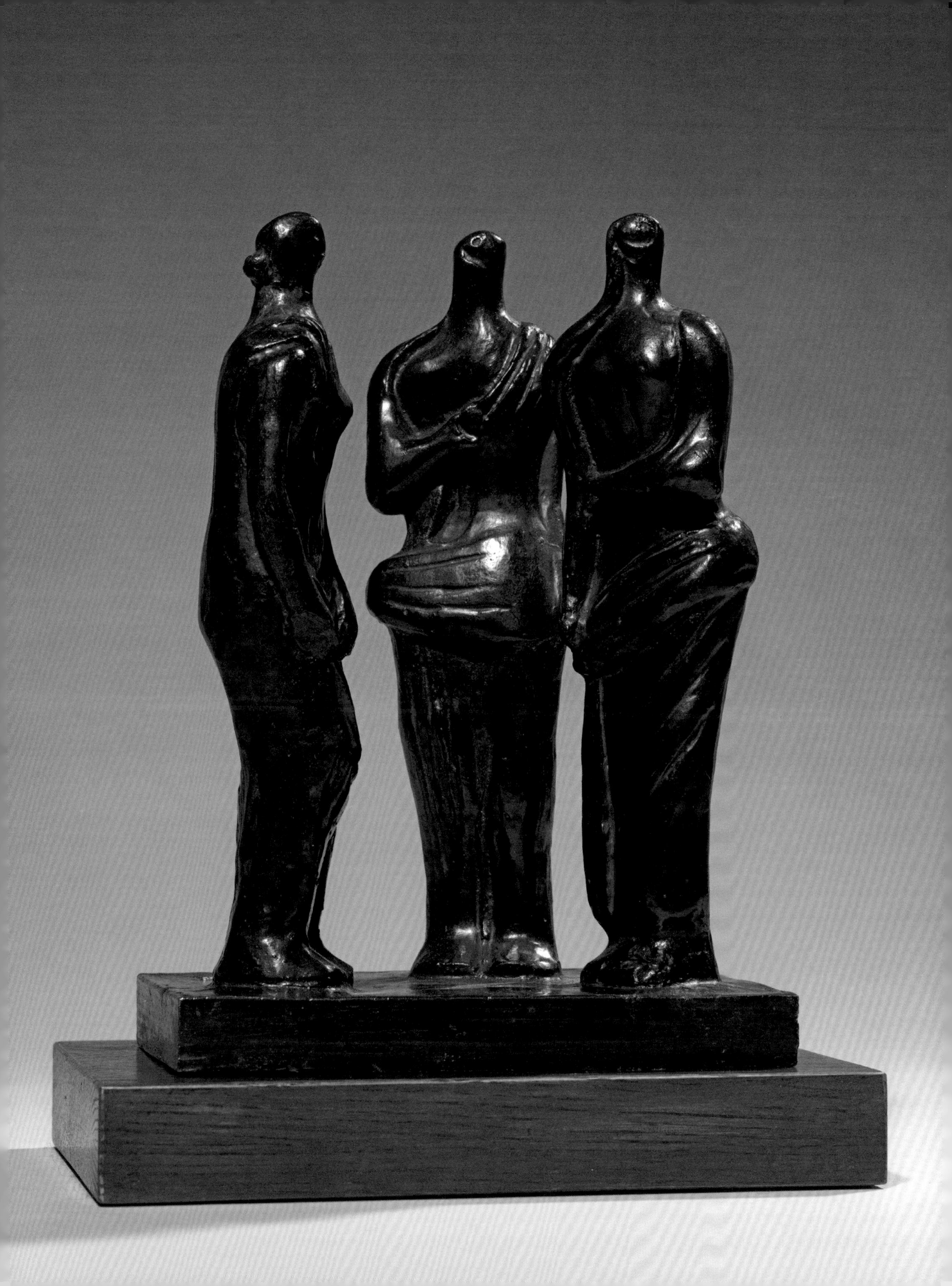

Henry Moore (1898-1986)

Standing Figure Relief No.2, 1960
Bronze
Signed lower right on the back of the figure
Numbered from the edition of 12
25.5 x 11.5 x 5 cms (10 x 4½ x 2 in)

Provenance
Dominion Gallery, Montreal, 1973
Private Collection, Canada

Literature
David Sylvester (ed.) and Herbert Read, *Henry Moore, Complete Sculpture*, vol. 3, no.461

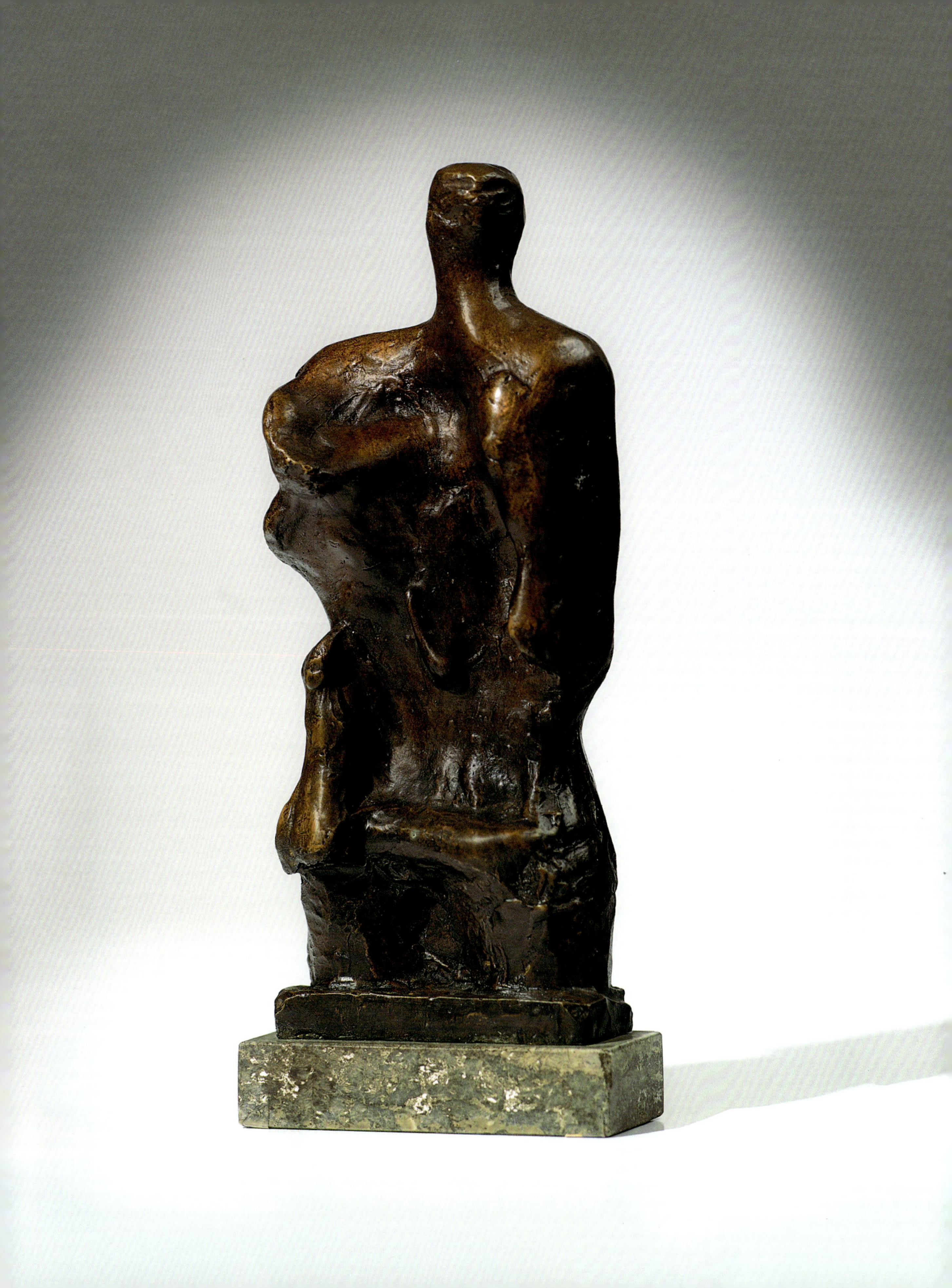

Henry Moore (1898-1986)

Reclining Figure: Holes, 1975
Bronze
Edition of 9
12.5 x 23.3 x 8 cms (5 x 9¼ x 3.5 in)

Provenance
The Artist
Fischer Fine Art, Ltd
Private Collection, UK, June 1976
Thence by descent

Literature
A. Bowness, ed., *Henry Moore, Sculpture and drawings*, vol. 5, Sculpture 1974-1980, London, 1983, no. 656, p. 20 & p. 21

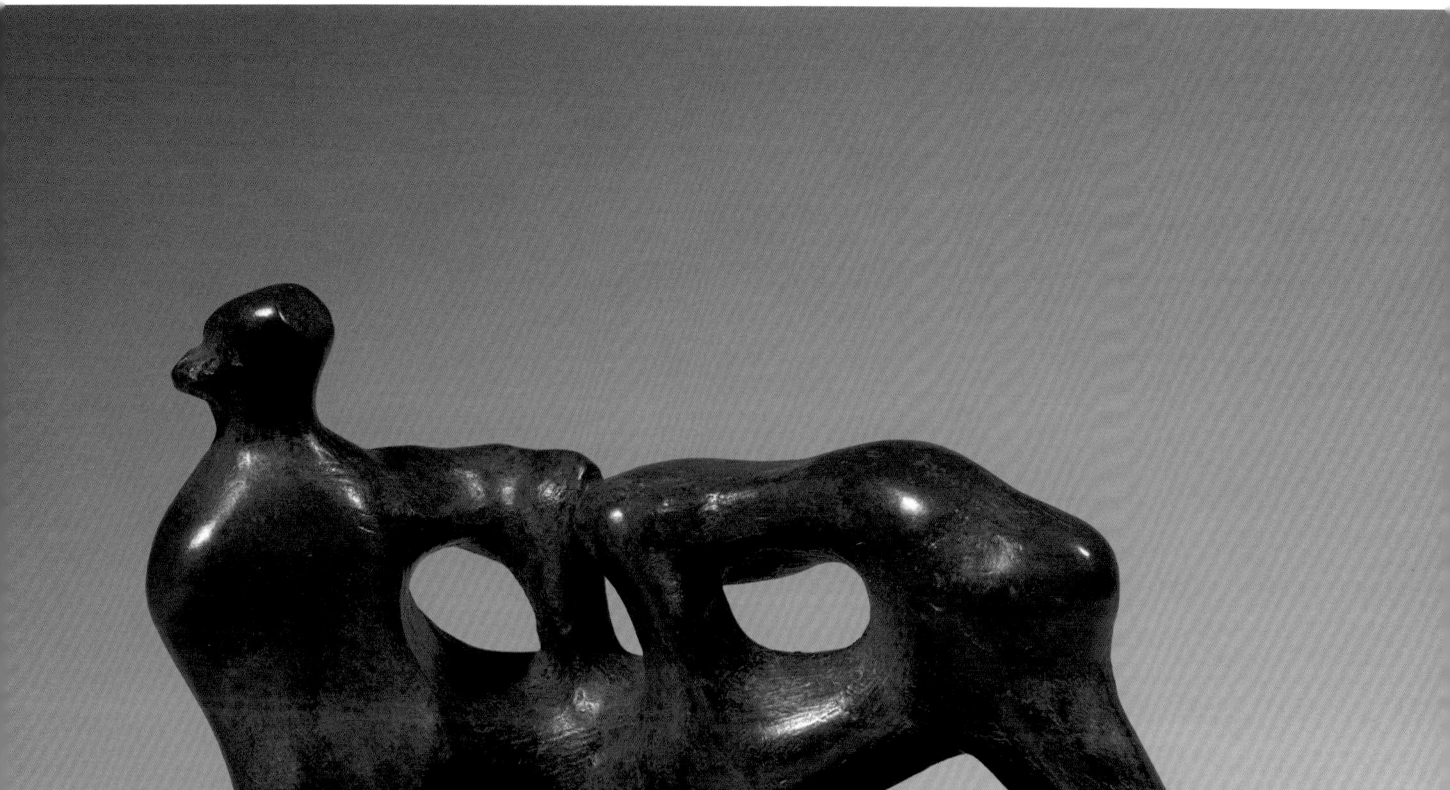

Barbara Hepworth (1903-1975)

Hepworth explained that 'the forms that have had special meaning for me since childhood have been the standing form (which is the translation of my feeling towards the human being standing in the landscape); the two forms (which is the tender relationship of one living thing beside another); and the closed form, such as the oval, spherical or pierced (sometimes incorporating colour) which translates for me the association and meaning of gesture in landscape; in the repose of say mother and child, or the feeling of the embrace of living things, either in nature or in the human spirit'.

The format of Tate Britain's recent exhibition of Hepworth's work from the 1920's to the early 1960's took the unusual, wise and enlightening curatorial decision to show her work in the context of her contemporaries in the 1920's, and to explore her working partnership with, or running in parallel alongside, her second husband Ben Nicholson, particularly in the subsequent decade. This brought out not so much her originality early on, as her belonging to a certain 1920's zeitgeist of restrained archaic or early classical sculpture – a version of, but not quite, a 'retour à l'ordre' of more expressive figurative sculpture than that seen in the restraint and monumentality of Maillol's work. The exhibits at the Tate showed how two generations overlapped: that of Jacob Epstein, Alan Durst, Eric Gill and Elsie Marion Henderson born around 1880, and herself and her first husband John Skeaping, Henry Moore, and Ursula Edgcumbe around 1900, with Gaudier-Brzeska in between the two.

By implication the exhibition demonstrated Hepworth's courage, determination and perseverance to pursue her vision in a male-dominated field, when an untold number of her female contemporaries appear to have more or less disappeared from sight. Even though sculptors such as Germaine Richier, Louise Nevelson, Elisabeth Frink and Louise Bourgeois would build successful careers after the Second World War, it would not be until a looser definition of sculpture and its materials, and the expansion of role models in the 1990's, that women sculptors might appear on an equal footing with, and in remotely equal numbers to, their male colleagues in public exhibitions.

Hepworth's career would sometimes run parallel, or intersect, with Moore's, as early on she tried out the pierced form in 1931, but then continued with the increasingly smoothed out, restrained figuration until her encounter with the work of Hans Arp and Piet Mondrian around 1933. Arp valued - that is to say permitted - the laws of chance to determine his reliefs, and allowed his sculpture to be shaped by the operation of his subconscious. The result may indeed suggest a plant or animal form, but this would be unintentional, leaving the reading to the viewer's imagination. Obviously not all shapes generated by the sculptor's hand would be preserved, as there had to be some mechanism of selection. 'Man must re-enter Nature' he once said, so nature-inspired, or nature-resembling works were preferred, and Hepworth seems to have taken up his enjoinder in such undulating forms and nestling shapes in her work, suggestive of natural growth or of a mother and child embracing. From the mid-1930's Nicholson's adoption of a Mondrian-esque disciplined geometry of circle and rectangle with limited colour spectrum accompanied Hepworth's paring down her own sculpture even further. This very purist, impersonal phase saw wood and marble forms restricted to pillar, egg, ball, and disc forms with few sharp edges, and the occasional homage to Giacometti's surrealist works of that decade. This rigorous abstraction would only loosen with the move to St Ives at the outbreak of war.

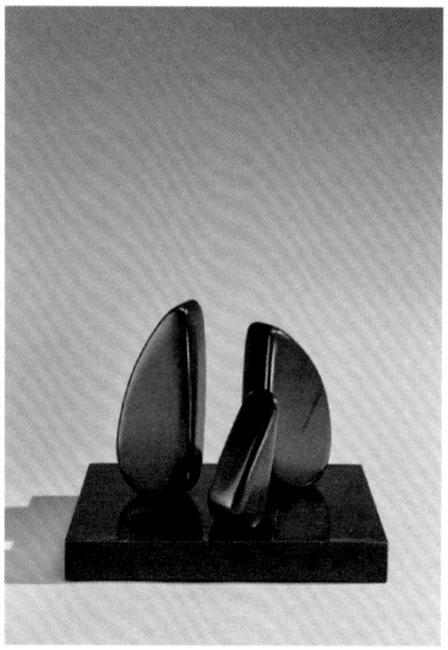

That move effectively severed her link with Moore, and liberated her work the better to express her own nature. She responded to the 'remarkable pagan landscape' of west Cornwall – 'a barbaric and magical countryside of rocky hills, fertile valleys and dynamic coastline' not unlike her native county, Yorkshire, with its rocky outcrops and weathered menhirs – which helped her to develop her ideas about the relationship of the human figure to the landscape. Unlike Moore, she did not make sketches for sculpture, but sought out forms for inspiration, linking her work to abstraction while striving for a classical form of harmony. She felt that 'working realistically replenishes one's love of life, humanity and the earth. Working abstractly seems to release one's personality and sharpen perceptions', confessing 'I hope to discover some absolute essence in sculptural terms giving the quality of human relationships'.

Selected to succeed Moore at the British Pavilion for the 1950 Venice Biennale, her visit provided a sort of epiphany on seeing such teeming human activity again, in the setting of this unique sea-bathed city. This led to several small and a few large 'clusters' of abstract pierced or monolithic vertical forms on a platform, and subsequently to an opening up of simple, often irregular shapes to bend and twist, expressive of, but without directly imitating forms in nature. A gift of African hardwood enabled her to carve a number of hollowed out, sensuous and tactile forms, some tensioned with string, with interiors coloured white for contrast. Although she had said, 'there are essential stone shapes and wood shapes that are impossible for me to disregard', after 1956 she could no longer carve exclusively in stone or wood. The demands of international exhibitions, and the time needed for carving obliged her to begin to use cut-sheet metal, and to make work in plaster for casting in bronze editions.

Her first public commission had only come in 1951 for the Festival of Britain, but after her Venice exhibition there would be an increasing number, such as for the Rietveldt Pavilion at Sonsbeek Park, which would later be transferred to the Rijksmuseum Kröller-Müller, and for the UN headquarters in New York, which called for work on a monumental scale. Maquettes of 'clustered' pierced forms such as 'Six forms on a circle' could be enlarged for public commissions, as could 'Three forms (extra Eye)', both executed in 1969. These are forerunners of what would be Hepworth's most ambitious and monumental group of forms to date, the 'Family of Man'; nine standing totem-like figures begun in the following year, realizing her long held dream of imposing bronzes scattered informally, like a family group walking across the landscape.

Above:
Three Forms on an Island, 1965
Slate, Unique. 30.5 x 25.4 x 24.1 cms (12 x 10 x 9 ½ in) (B 390)

Barbara Hepworth (1903-1975)

Six Forms on a Circle, 1967
Polished Bronze
From the edition of 7 cast from a slate model
Signed, dated and numbered from the edition of 7 on upper surface of base.
Inscribed "Morris Singer Foundry London" on side of base.
33.7 x 60 x 60 cms (13¼ x 23½ x 23½ in)

Provenance
Marlborough Fine Art, London
Private Collection, USA
Private Collection, UK

Exhibited
Barbara Hepworth, Tate Gallery, London, April-May 1968, No. 183, another cast
Barbara Hepworth: New Sculpture and Drawings, Gimpel Gallery, New York, 1969, No. 5, another cast illus. in catalogue

Literature
The Complete Sculpture of Barbara Hepworth, editied by Alan Bowness, number 454, plate 174

The artist's cast was exhibited at Tate, 1968 and is now at the entrance to the Hepworth Wakefield.

The sculpture is on a turntable and rotates. At the time the artist wrote:
"I began to get more turntables and to try and assess my own changing movements in relation to the sun."

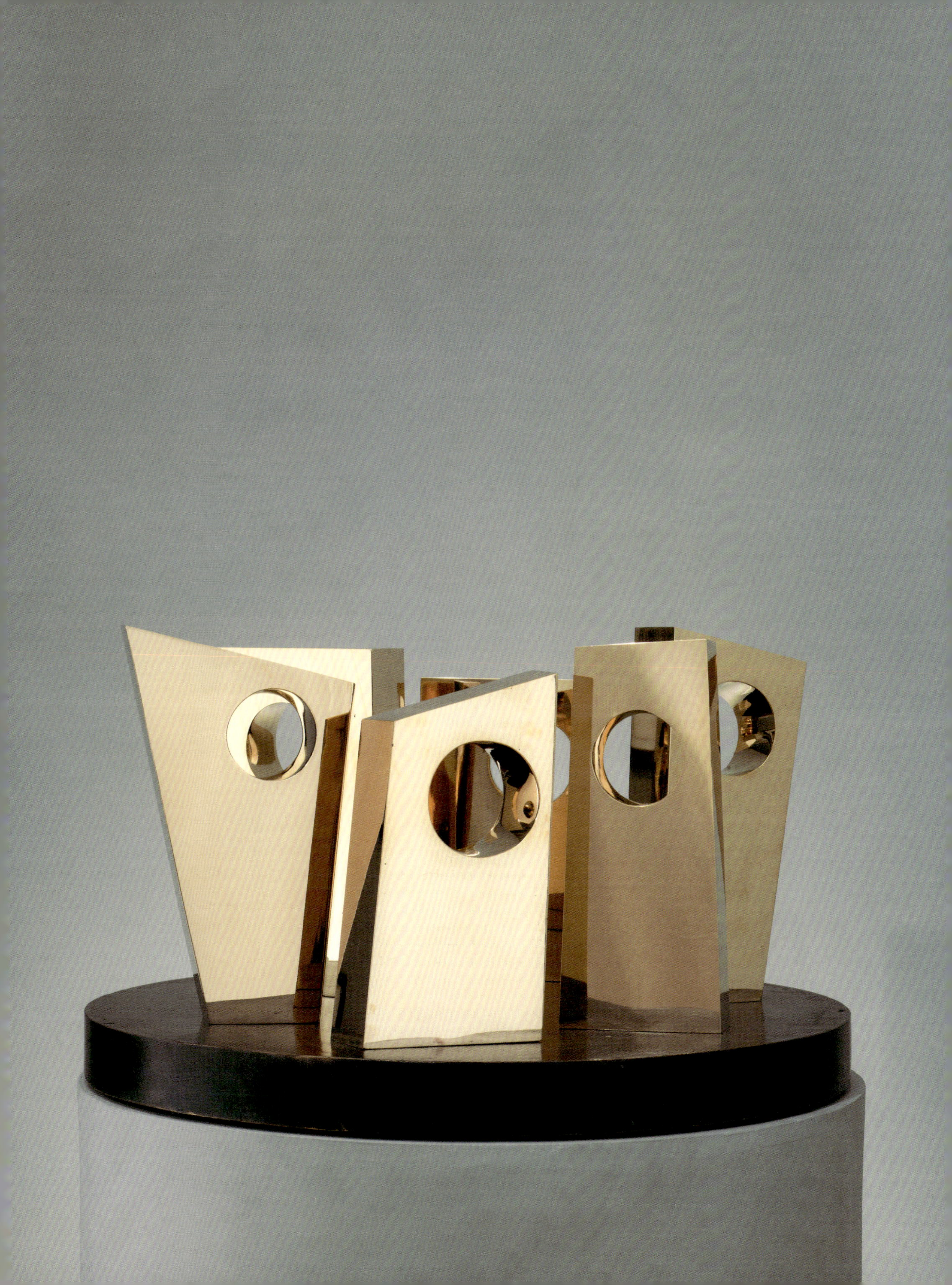

Barbara Hepworth (1903-1975)

Three Forms (Extra Eye), 1969
Bronze
Signed, dated and numbered from the edition of 9 on the base
Also initialled with the foundry mark for Morris Singer, `MS'
22.4 x 20.2 x 15.1 cms (8¾ x 8 x 6 in)

Provenance
The Artist
Gimpel fils, 1972
Private Collection, USA

Exhibited
London, Marlborough Fine Art, *Barbara Hepworth Recent work, Sculpture, Paintings, Prints,* February March 1970, no. 26

Literature
Exhibition catalogue, *Barbara Hepworth Recent work Sculpture, Paintings, Prints, London,* Marlborough Fine Art, 1970, no. 26, p. 30.
The Complete Sculpture of Barbara Hepworth 1960-1969, edited by A. Bowness, published by Lund Humphries, 1971, pp. 48-49, no. 487

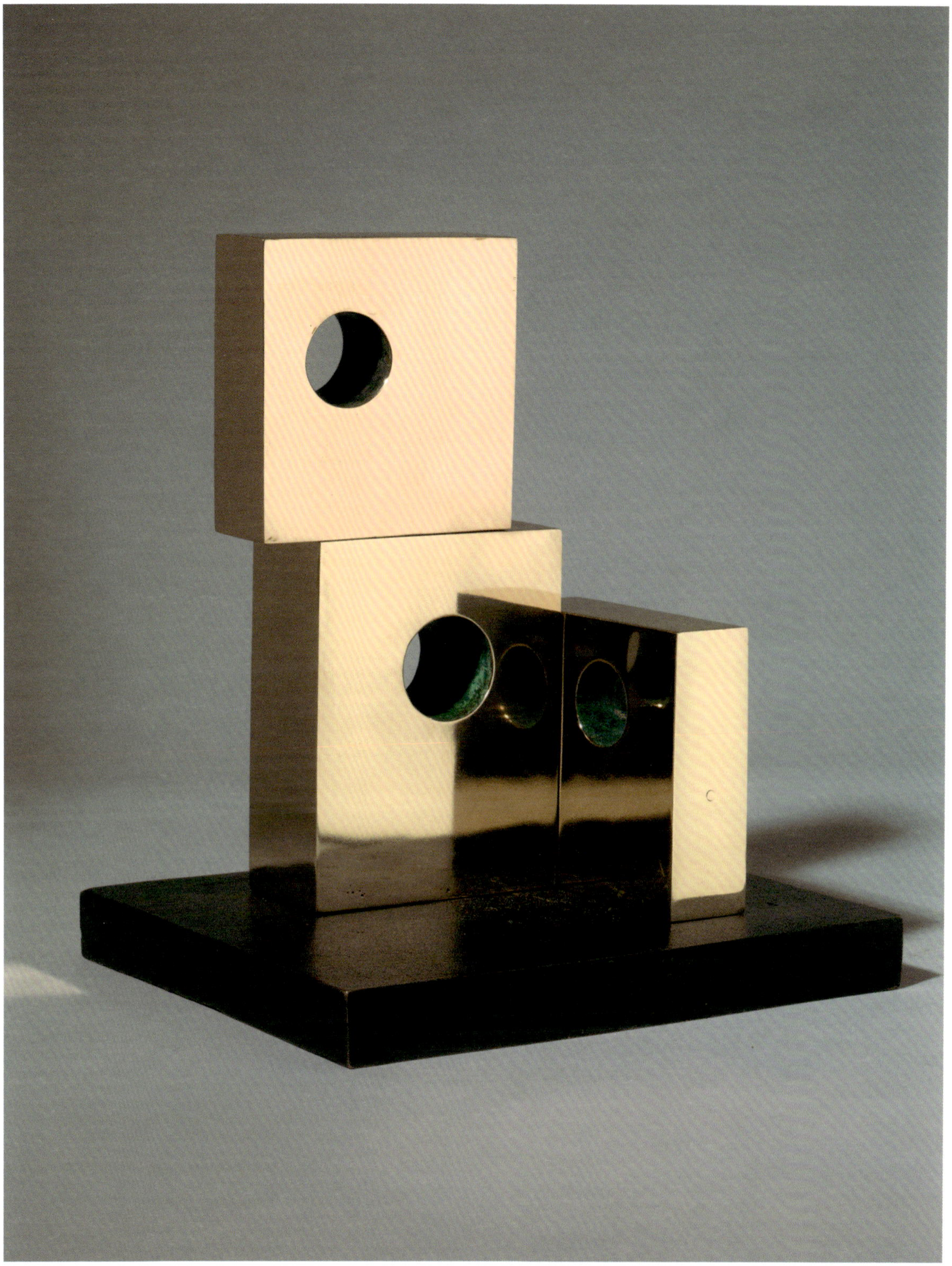

Reg Butler (1913-1981)

Was it inevitable that Herbert Read's pithy but unintentional epithet (taken out of context) of 'the geometry of fear', with which he introduced the work of the post-war generation of British sculptors including Butler at the 1952 Venice Biennale, would eventually be contested? The paragraph in question read: *"These new images belong to the iconography of despair, or of defiance; and the more innocent the artist, the more effectively he transmits the collective guilt. Here are images of flight, of ragged claws 'scuttling across the floors of silent seas', of excoriated flesh, frustrated sex, the geometry of fear. Gone forever is the serenity, the monumental calm, that a Winckelmann had imposed on the formal imagination of Europe".*

As a well-known and highly respected writer on art, and friend of so many British artists over the previous thirty years, Read's poetic characterization interpreted a certain pessimistic mood of the new nuclear age, also given the state of the current cold war in the West, and the Korean war in the East. Read chose not to allude to the slightly forced optimism of the previous year's Festival of Britain (at which work by most of these young sculptors was also seen), or the impending, hoped-for dawn of a new 'Elizabethan Age'. But he also – understandably, given the context – glossed over the very different origins, aims and styles of each sculptor and possibly – more significantly – did not refer to the broader recent history of British, not to speak of continental (meaning mainly French), art debates and practices.

That European art after the Second World War experienced a rupture with previous philosophies and styles was obvious and indeed inevitable (see 'Afterthought', below). After the isolation of the war, London immediately tried to reconnect with the continent, mounting major exhibitions of Picasso, Matisse and Klee in 1945. Nor were the exhibition programmes of the reformulated Arts Council (grown out of the wartime CEMA) and the new Institute of Contemporary Art restricted to British art alone. Some British artists and critics travelled to France, a few stayed for a while, and even fewer travelled further afield, foreign currency restrictions permitting.

But the record is incomplete - and to a certain extent untraceable – on who met whom, who saw what, and who read what, if indeed this is relevant to understanding how and why artists came to be making the work they did.

Tall Woman, 1950
Forged and welded iron
Unique
103 x 22 x 21 cms (40½ x 8¾ x 8¼ in)

Provenance
Private Collection, UK

Literature
The Sculpture of Reg Butler, Margaret Garlake, published by The Henry Moore Foundation in association with Lund Humphries, 2006, no. 62, p.124 (RB38)

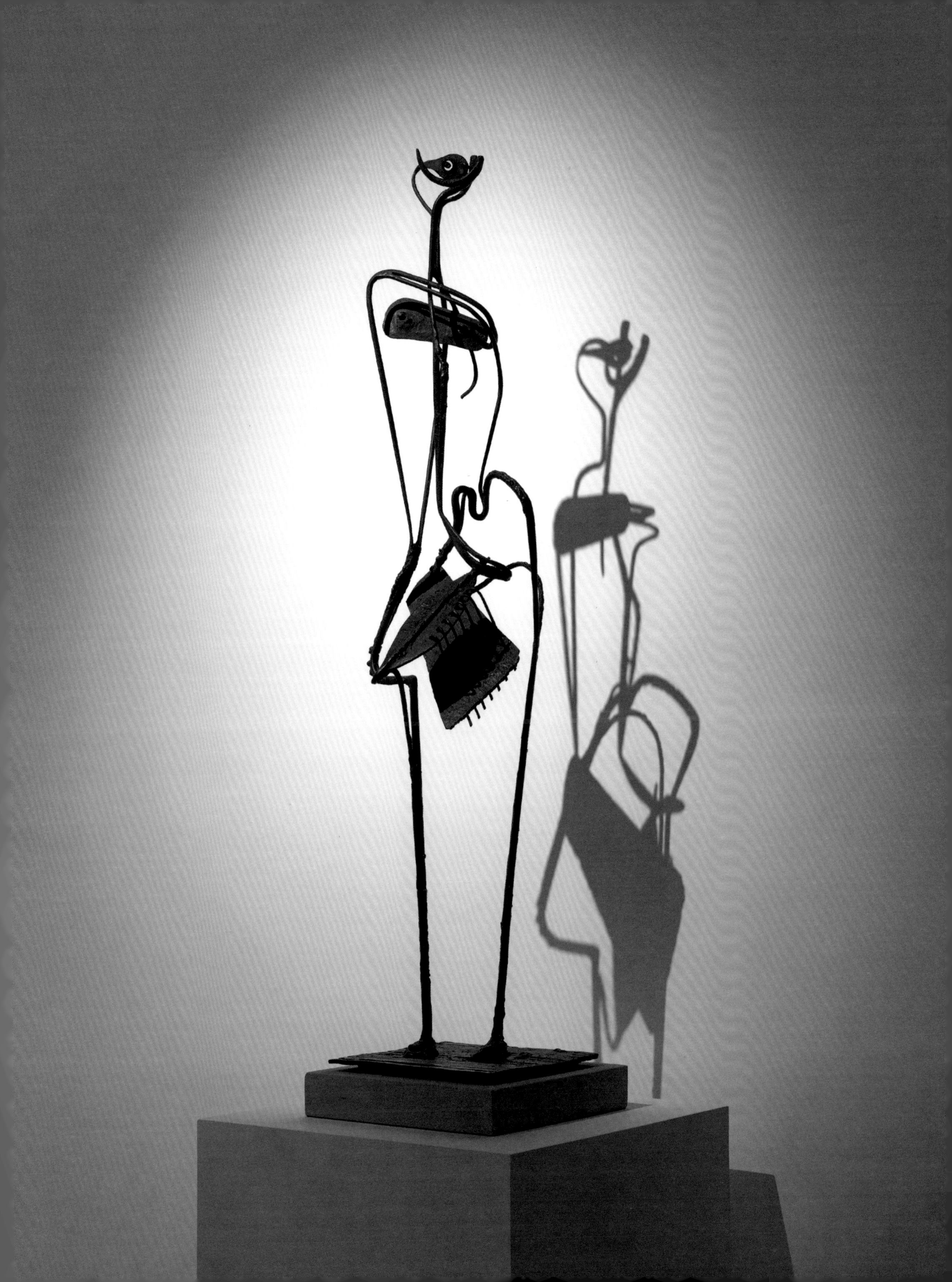

Reg Butler (1913-1981)

The mere record of which exhibitions were held where, who lived and worked where, or which important modern art magazines were in circulation, provides a skeleton framework for a history, but does little to help connect the dots. Artists may overlook, forget or deny the impact of an encounter, so the account may become inaccurate – even if such a concept might exist that was capable of measuring 'accuracy' about artistic creativity.

In the context of this new generation of British sculptors, a follow-through from the neo-Romantics is sometimes downplayed. Not only their spiky entanglements in the English countryside, but the towering presence of their 'mentor' Graham Sutherland, whose famous paintings of a pathos-bathed crucifixion, sharp-clawed thorn trees, and sinister standing forms at the end of the war, anticipated the appearance of some of the new sculptors' work. Sutherland's reputation had not yet been overtaken by that of Francis Bacon, though the latter's new start with the 'Three figures at the base of a crucifixion' and his 'Painting 1946' already reflected scenes of aggression, horror or mutilation that many of the young sculptors themselves would have witnessed or seen depicted during their own war service. And then there were the pre-war cages, spiked forms and openwork seen in Giacometti's surrealist constructions, and Picasso's cut-out and welded iron sculptures around 1930 which, like Giacometti's, had been reproduced in magazines such as 'Minotaure' and 'Cahiers d'Art' which the patron and collector Peter Watson – one of the founders of the I.C.A. alongside Read and Roland Penrose – may have owned and shown around. This is not to overlook the suggestions or connections that Read himself, or someone like the dynamic young and peripatetic critic David Sylvester, may have offered to those sculptors whom he met. Sylvester was one of the first British writers on art to engage with the Paris art scene post-war, meeting the two most talked about figures, Giacometti and Dubuffet, around 1946-47. As another famous critic, Lawrence Alloway, later summed up those early post-war years: 'The art world in Europe in the late 40's and early 50's must be pictured as full of artists out of touch with one another, conscious of waiting to see Pollock or Giacometti or Dubuffet for the first time'.

Turning to Butler, it is not without significance that he, like Chadwick, was in reality 'self-taught'. By dint of his age and experience, he could hardly be described by Read as 'innocent'. Unlike Moore and Hepworth who had studied at art college, Butler had been a qualified architect before the war, and had performed his war service as a blacksmith making tools and repairing agricultural machinery, so was well acquainted with working, forging and welding iron.

Manipulator 1, 1953
Shell bronze
Unique
Stamped with monogram on the base
76.2 x 26 x 23 cms (30 x 10¼ x 9 in)

Provenance
Private Collection, UK

Exhibited
Hanover 1954, no.20
Curt Valentin 1955, no. 18

Literature
The Sculpture of Reg Butler, Margaret Garlake, published by The Henry Moore Foundation in association with Lund Humphries, 2006, no. 124, p.137 (RB104)

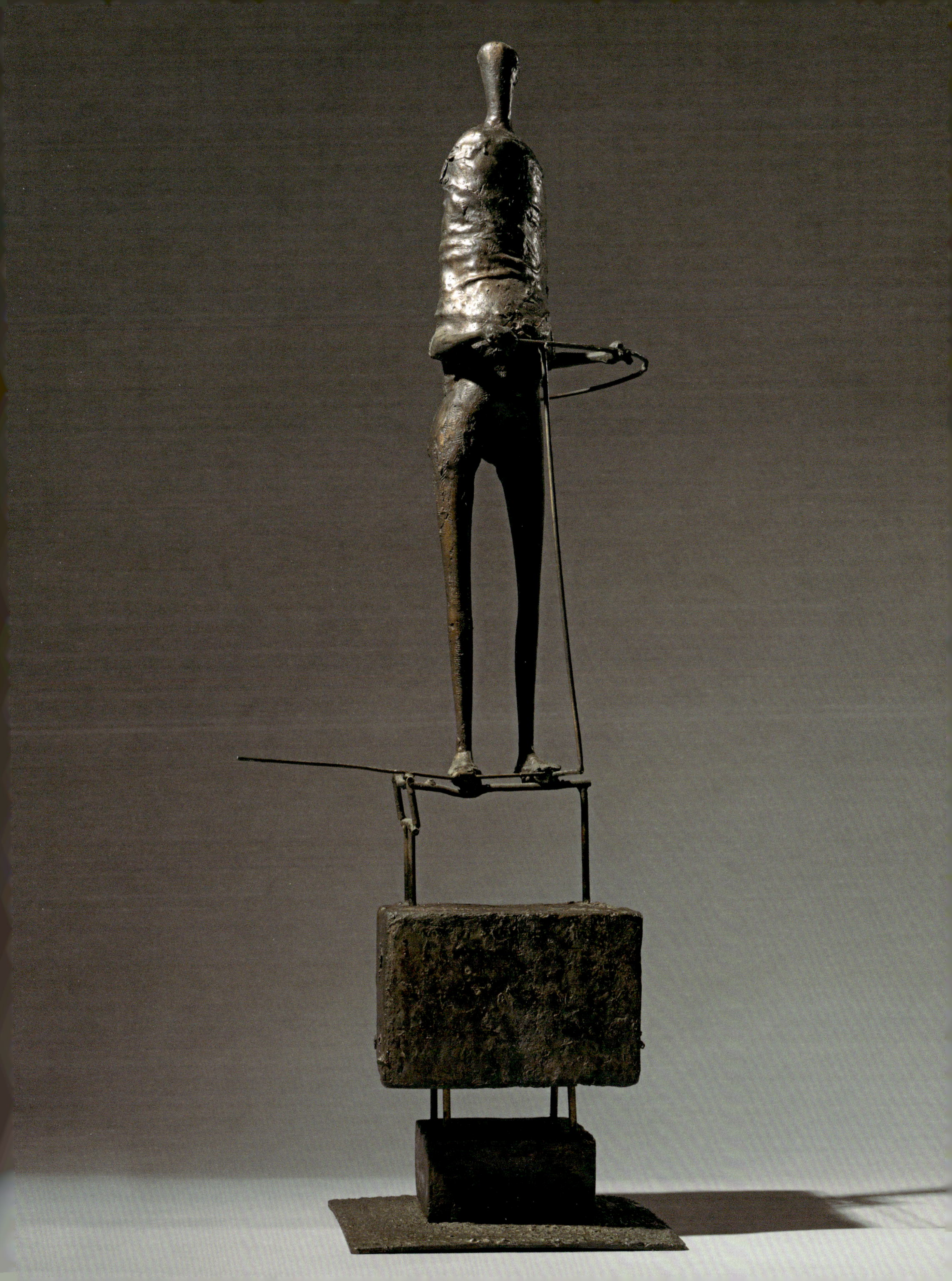

Reg Butler (1913-1981)

He had begun to sculpt in 1944, even spending a brief period in 1948 as an assistant to Moore. The sight of Britain's spindly, often damaged radar towers at the end of the war appears to have suggested to him creating transparent sculptural forms as a way of escaping from the influence of Moore's example. However, the series of forged and welded iron sculptures such as 'Tall Woman' still share Moore's subject matter, although the technique Butler now adopted had more distant roots in Julio Gonzalez' collaboration on sculptures with Picasso around 1930. They too were working with welded rods and cut sheets of iron, in essence creating drawings in space with metal outlines. No doubt this filiform technique of assembling the bare bones of a sculpture also echoed sights of wartime destruction; tortured steel skeletons of buildings revealed by bomb destruction. At the same time the bones and sinews of the figure alluded to structures and organic growth patterns found in the natural world.

Butler's exhibition at the Hanover Gallery in 1949 of both vertical and horizontal sculptures in this style met with great success, and he was invited to be the first Gregory Fellow in Sculpture at Leeds (E.C.Gregory was the director of Lund Humphries art publishers, based in Leeds, and an art collector and founding member of the I.C.A.). This would ensure Butler's inclusion in the British Council's more challenging exhibition at the 1952 Venice Biennale, 'New Aspects of British Sculpture', after the muted reception given to Barbara Hepworth's exhibit in 1950. All the chosen sculptors of the post-war generation included in that Venice showing feature in our exhibition. That 1952 British entry also included paintings by Edward Wadsworth and Graham Sutherland, the latter providing some parallels in painting to the sculptors' work, with the aggressive, contorted forms he found in nature.

It was the I.C.A. that devised and organized the famous international competition for a 'Monument to the Unknown Political Prisoner', which Butler won in the following year from among some 3,500 submissions. This proved to be a stylistic and reputational turning point for the sculptor, cementing his fame among artists across Europe and America, but also eliciting an unsympathetic response from the British public. His design envisaged a triangular platform (the only solid-sheet element in the design) raised on stilts, on which hollow frame structures and a tall vertical pole were anchored. However, the similarity to a prisoner-of-war camp watchtower was not missed and, sadly in the end, after years of delays and wrangling, the monument planned for siting on the border of the east and west zones of Berlin was never erected. It would mark the end of Butler's 'open work' sculpture when, searching for more tangible forms, he invented a thin-shell bronze technique of his own, as seen in 'Descent' 1953.

£20,000

Study for Girl with Vest, 1955
Bronze
Edition of 8
23.6 x 11.6 x 4.2 cms (9¼ x 4½ x 1¾ in)

Provenance
Estate of the artist
Gallery Pangolin, Chalford, 2006
Private Collection, USA

Exhibited
ICA, Christmas Fair, 1955
Hanover Gallery, cat 16, 1957

Literature
The Sculpture of Reg Butler, Margaret Garlake, published by The Henry Moore Foundation in association with Lund Humphries, 2006, no. 156, p.144 (RB134)

This work earned its title with the first of Butler's series of what he termed 'manipulated torsos', catching and twisting the hollow thin-shell bronze torso in a web of rods at the bottom of a vertiginous angled pole. The theme of entrapment chimed with the cage structures of Giacometti's earlier work, and also with Germaine Richier's contemporary animal- or insect-like figures, they too, immobilized by rods attached to their limbs. Although his torsos would gradually gain more human features, their hands or feet would continue to be ensnared by rods, denying them full human verisimilitude until the end of that decade, when he turned to solid bronze casting.

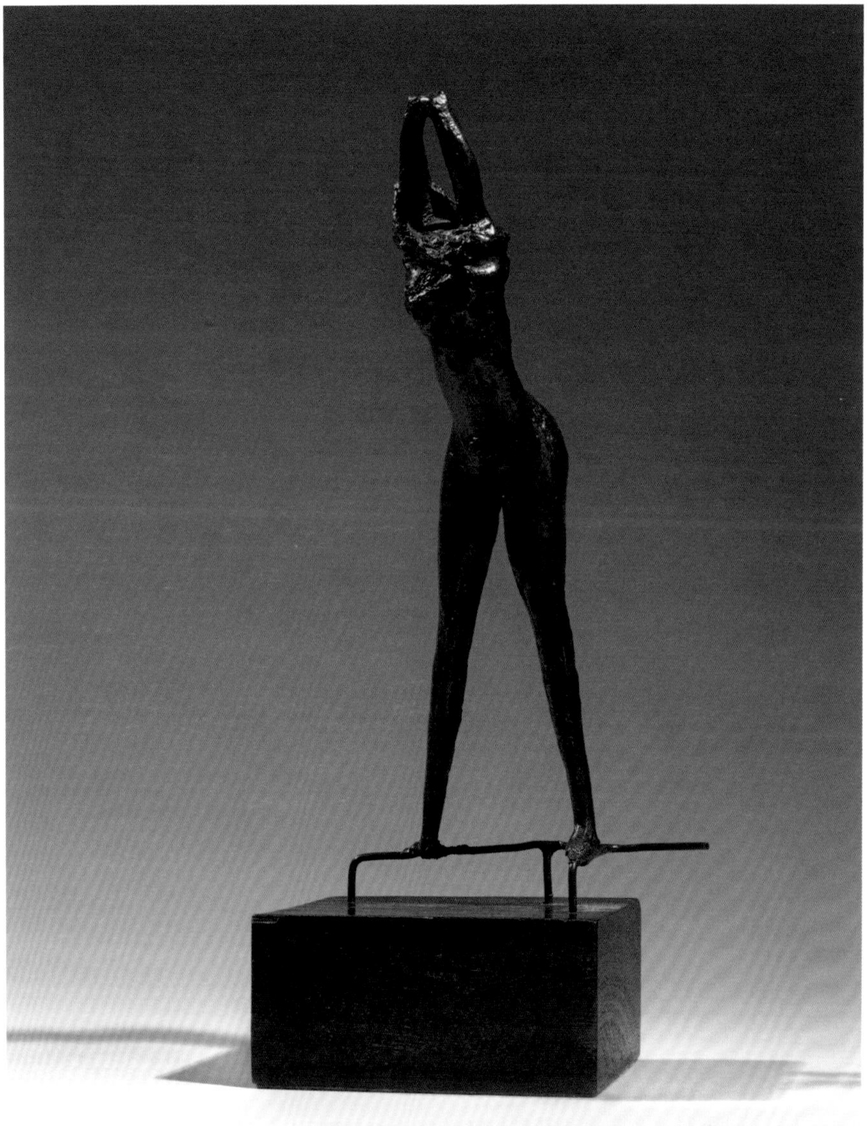

Reg Butler (1913-1981)

Study for Girl with a Vest, 1959
Bronze
Edition of 8
Inscribed with artist's monogramme and marked with the foundry name on base,
Fondeur Susse Frères, Paris
57.8 x 13.3 x 11 cms (22¾ x 5¼ x 4¼ in)

Provenance
Private Collection, UK

Exhibited
1960, London, Hanover Gallery, *Reg Butler: Sculpture*, cat. 28
1962, New York, Pierre Matisse Gallery, *Reg Butler: Recent Sculpture 1959-1962*, cat. 12 1964, The University of Leeds, *The Gregory Fellows*, Arts Council, cat. 4

Literature
Melville, Motif, no. 6, 1961
The Sculpture of Reg Butler, Margaret Garlake, published by The Henry Moore Foundation in association with Lund Humphries, 2006, no. 196, p.155 (RB196)

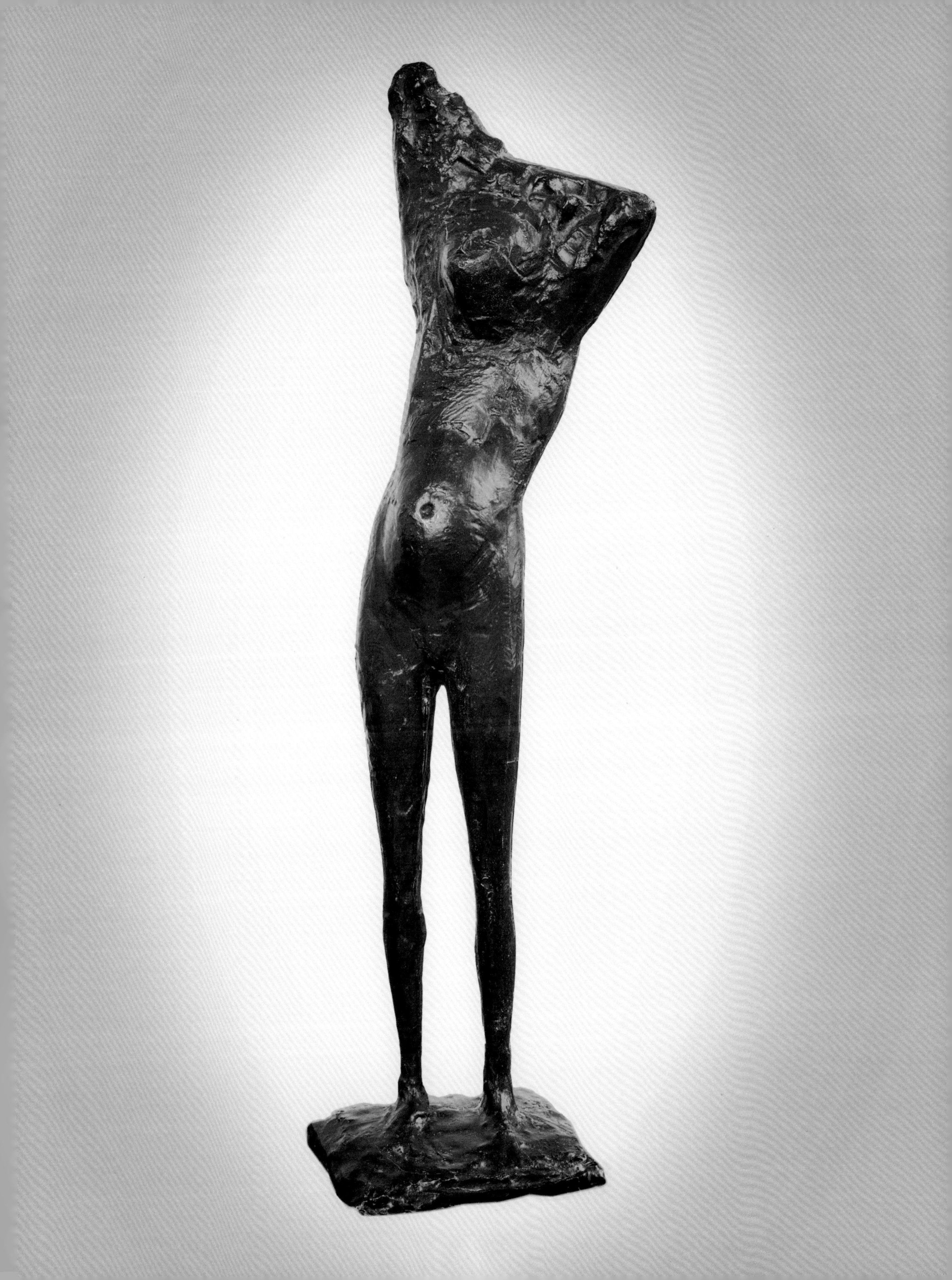

Lynn Chadwick (1914-2003)

International recognition came early to Chadwick, due in part to significant early support from the British Council leading to his inclusion in the pivotal Venice Biennales of 1952 and 1956. He won the International Prize for Sculpture at the 1956 Biennale, when it was expected to go to Giacometti (who eventually won it in 1962), a remarkable achievement for a sculptor who, like Butler, was 'self-taught' and who had an exhibiting career of scarcely a single decade. But in truth Chadwick had a wish to become an artist from the early 1930's, but had been persuaded by his father to pursue furniture and textile design and architectural draughtmanship in the Depression years. After war service as a Fleet Air Arm pilot, he resumed working with a design firm and began to make mobiles for trade shows in wood, perspex and aluminium. Enrolling on a welding course with the British Oxygen Company (as Butler would also do) in 1950 assisted him in producing two signal and substantial mobiles in 1951, 'Dragonfly' and 'Fisheater', later acquired by the Tate Gallery. In essence these demonstrated his difference from, and his different pathway to, mobile sculpture, compared with that of Alexander Calder, to whom Chadwick's work of this period has been misleadingly compared.

While Calder usually hand-cut rounded and oval painted shapes, and spaced them out in evocative patterns on simple wire frameworks, Chadwick's geometric, interlocking shapes appeared to be cut from a single sheet and, in the 1951 mobiles, anchored by an elaborate, rigid, constructed framework of iron rods, suggestive of the insect or marine form of its title. In the following year, developing this constructed framework of forged and welded rods brought his sculpture down to earth on poised, skeletal legs, foreshadowing the future character of his work. 'Diamond Lil' and the several variants of the large 'Inner Eye' that would be purchased by Alfred Barr for the Museum of Modern Art in New York, introduced quasi-modelled iron sheets sheltering a solid glass fragment held in the claws of iron rods.

Mobile, 1952
Iron and steel
Unique
Width: 125 cms (49¼ in)

Provenance
Gift from the Artist to the present owner

Exhibited
Lynn Chadwick, Osborne Samuel, February - March 2011, p. 21

Literature
Lynn Chadwick Sculpture, Dennis Farr & Eva Chadwick, published by Lund Humphries, no.78, p.80

Originally the mobile was counter balanced by a large iron disc. The artist removed this larger element once it was installed in the home of the family to whom it was gifted.

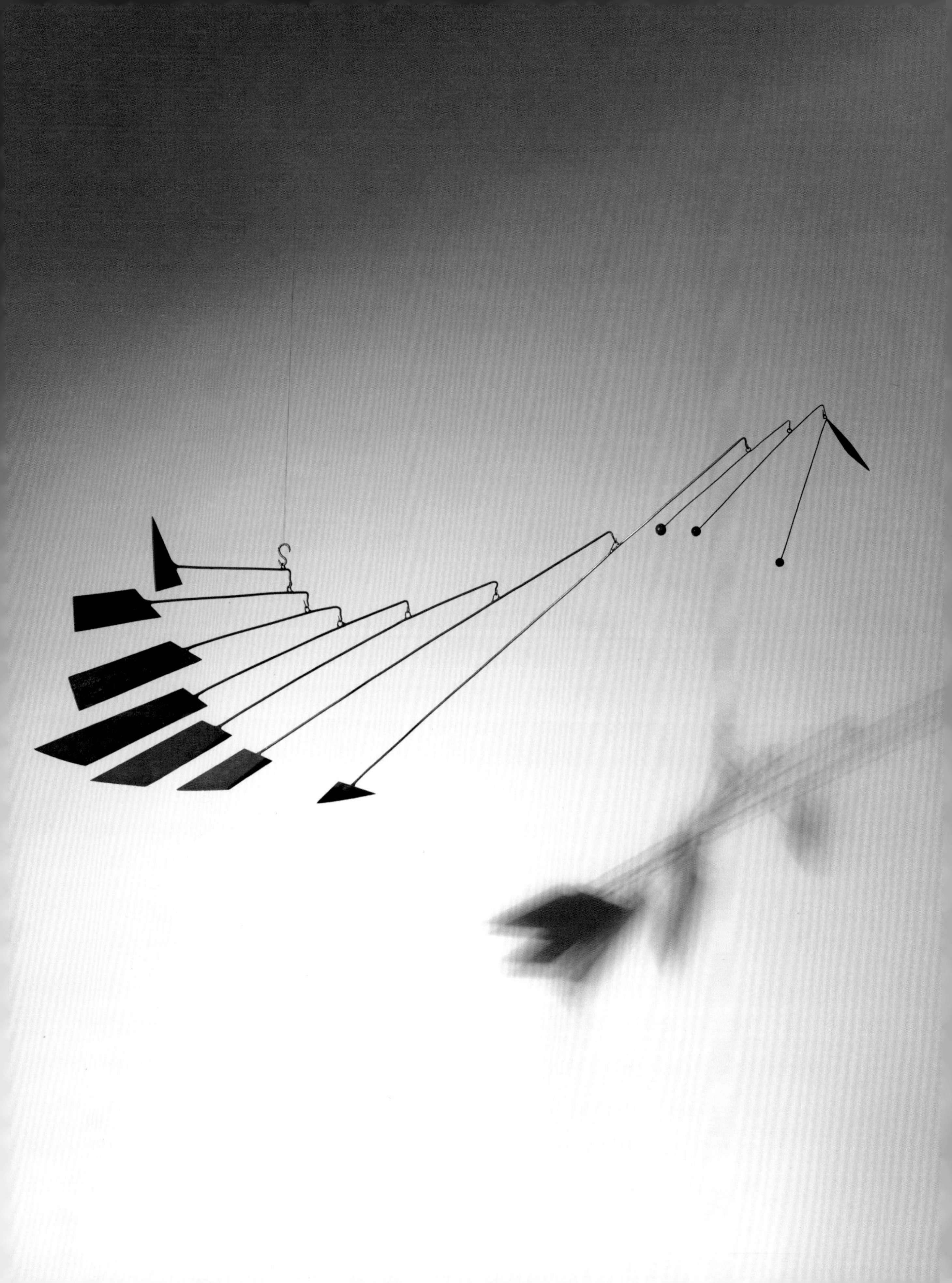

Lynn Chadwick (1914-2003)

In this brief phase Chadwick could be said to come closest to Read's 'geometry of fear', these works suggesting the remains of a delicate living thing which had been pared down to its bare bone structure, revealing a mysterious diamond-hard transparent core, whose very origin and function were unknowable.

Sculptures on a structure of iron rods, lifted off the ground by thin supports that seem to defy gravity and risk toppling over, were the antithesis, and in a sense a riposte to, the grounded quality of Moore's weighty reclining figures and the smooth carved surfaces of Hepworth's resting abstract forms. The next step for Chadwick would be to give more body to these exposed structures, at first with cut and shaped iron sheets, but eventually with a new sculptural material that he had discovered: a mixture of powdered iron and cement called Stolit which, when mixed with water, hardened to the strength of bronze. Chadwick explained how welding the rods provided the basis for the work that triumphed at Venice: 'The actual technique acted as a guide, and gave its character to the work .... I do not analyse my work intellectually. When I start to work I wait until I feel what I want to do, and I know how I'm doing by the presence or lack of a rhythmic impulse. I think that the attempt to analyse the ability to draw ideas from their subconscious source would almost certainly interfere with that ability'. Early work in this new phase still held echoes of insect or bird behaviour - parading, pecking, flaunting – which remnants would occasionally reappear as features in subjects such as the 'Winged Figures'. 'Dancers' and 'Teddy Boy and Girl', the former with its counterpoint movement, the latter with the upright confidence of cheeky parading, suggested an insight into the parallels of human and animal behavior underlined, too, by the sexual suggestion of a work such as 'Conjunction'.

Diamond Lil, 1952
Iron and glass
Unique
Height: 38 cms (15 in)

Provenance
Private Collection, UK

Exhibited
College Art Gallery, Gloucester (with John Piper), Sept. - Oct. 1960
Lynn Chadwick, Osborne Samuel, February - March 2011, p. 18 & 19

Literature
Lynn Chadwick Sculpture, Dennis Farr & Eva Chadwick, published by Lund Humphries, no.88, p.75
Architectural Design 29/4 (Apr. 1959). 151 (as 'Composition in iron and glass 1952')

Diamond Lil was the nickname of Lilian Somerville, the head of the Fine Art Department from 1948-1970, whose responsibilities included the selection of artists for the Venice Biennales. She was trained as a painter, so her sympathies lay with the artists – she was a particularly strong advocate for many of the post war sculptors.

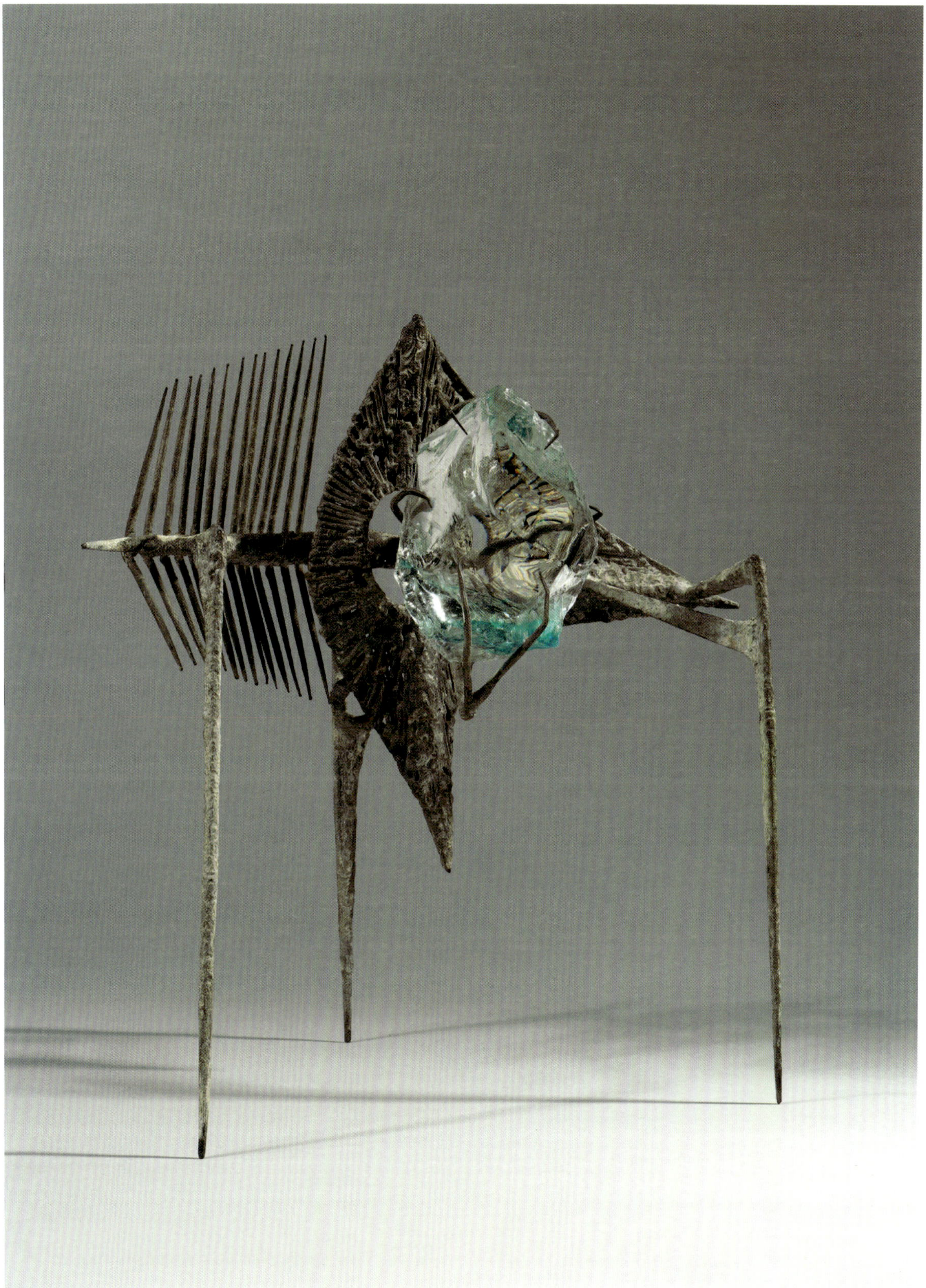

Lynn Chadwick (1914-2003)

'Teddy Boy and Girl' and similar vertical figure groups shared with some of Chadwick's contemporaries the miniaturization of the head – in effect a counterbalance to the reduction of the lower limbs into points. But as his figures spread out with wings in the 'Strangers' and 'Watchers' series, the suggestion of an unfamiliar or even hostile presence seemed to need the identity of a purposeful figure with sentience who would fulfill the role of intruding or observing. These figures acquired heads as heavy and strong as their torsos, and were rendered immobile by the expedient of a pedestal. Were these figures a subconscious reflection of the Cold War atmosphere of spying and surveillance which came to a head with the Cuban Missile Crisis? Its eventual peaceful resolution coincided with a brief interlude when Chadwick turned to working with found iron elements welded into standing forms in his 'Insider' and 'Indicator' series. Owing to the imperfections he had detected with Stolit when exposed to the English weather over the longer term, and also in response to demand for his work, in 1959 he began to have works cast in bronze. After the welded iron works, in 1963 he would return to bronze casting for the rest of his working life, with only rare forays to experiment with stainless steel, after the invitation he had once taken up to visit and make a work with the Italian steel company Italsider in 1962. Thereafter Chadwick's work continued to show what he described as a 'deliberate continuity'. His figurative structures evolve, with the iconic triangular and square heads immediately recognizable, and a considerable importance attached to the relationship between figures, the dynamic tension created by the juxtaposition of male and female figures. This challenge occupied the artist for the rest of his career.

Mobile, 1952
Steel and Brass
Unique
35 x 79 x 23.8 cms (13¾ x 31 x 9¼ in)

Provenance
Gift from the Artist
(Lynn Chadwick's notebook states the it was gifted to 'Madeleine ill in bed, May 18th 1952')

Literature
Lynn Chadwick Sculptor, Dennis Farr & Eva Chadwick, published by Lund Humphries, no. 77, p.80

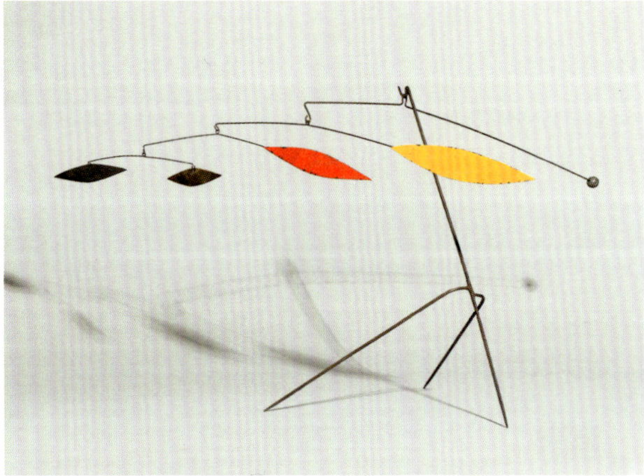

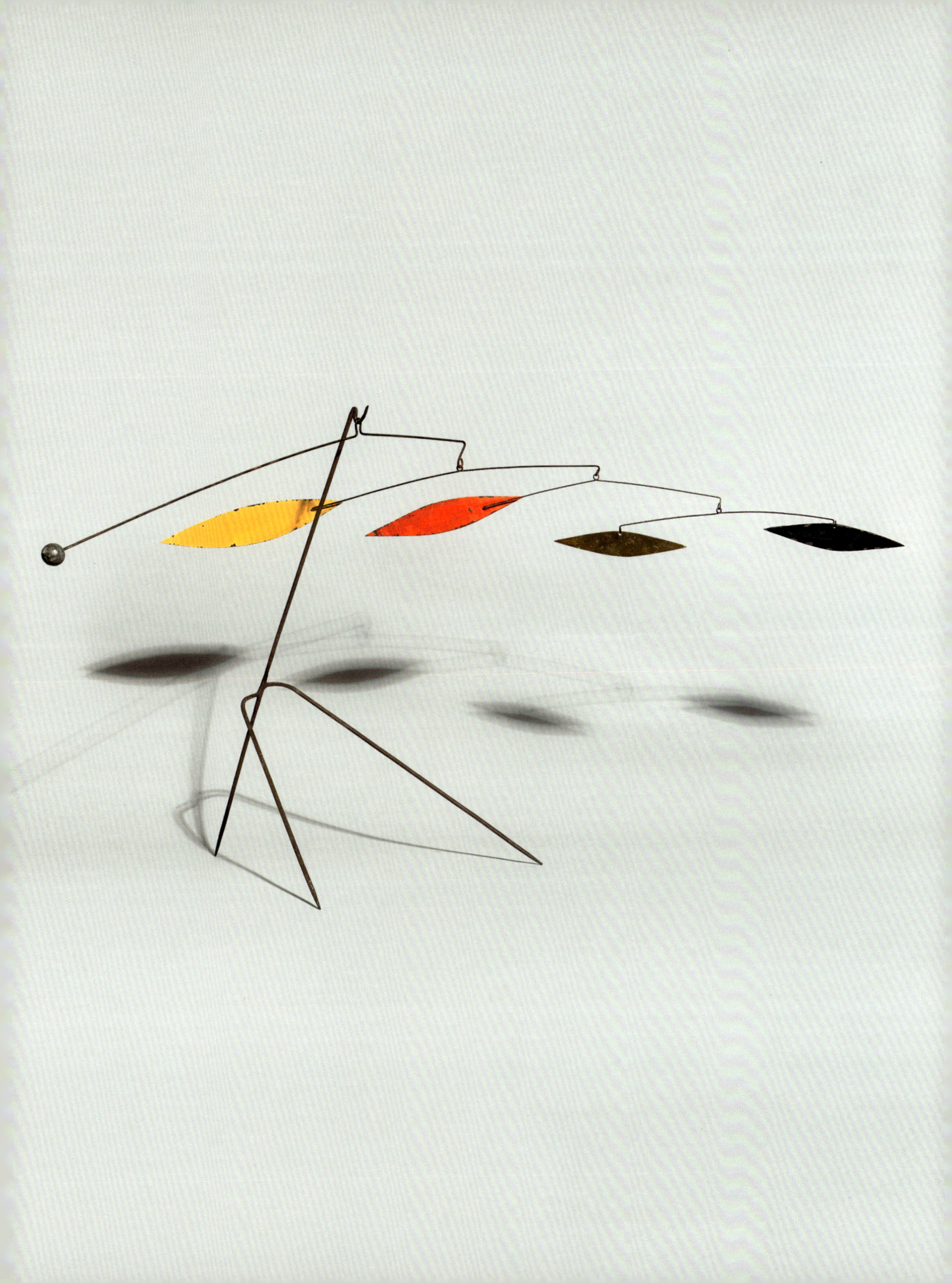

Lynn Chadwick (1914-2003)

Second Stranger, 1956
Bronze
Edition of 9
Cast by Pangolin Editions, January 1987
Height: 45 x 26 x 17 cms (18 ½ x 10 ¼ x 6 ¾ in)

Provenance
Estate of the artist
Gallery Pangolin, Chalford
Acquired from the above circa 2006

Literature
Lynn Chadwick (exhibition catalogue), Caracas, Museo de Arte Contemporáneo Sofía Imber, 1990-91, p. 28
Lynn Chadwick (exhibition catalogue), Toyama, Museum of Modern Art; Saitama, Museum of Modern Art; Hakone, Hakone Open Air Museum & Kyoto, Museum of Kyoto, 1991, p. 24
Lynn Chadwick Sculptor, Dennis Farr & Eva Chadwick, published by Lund Humphries, no. 189, p.118

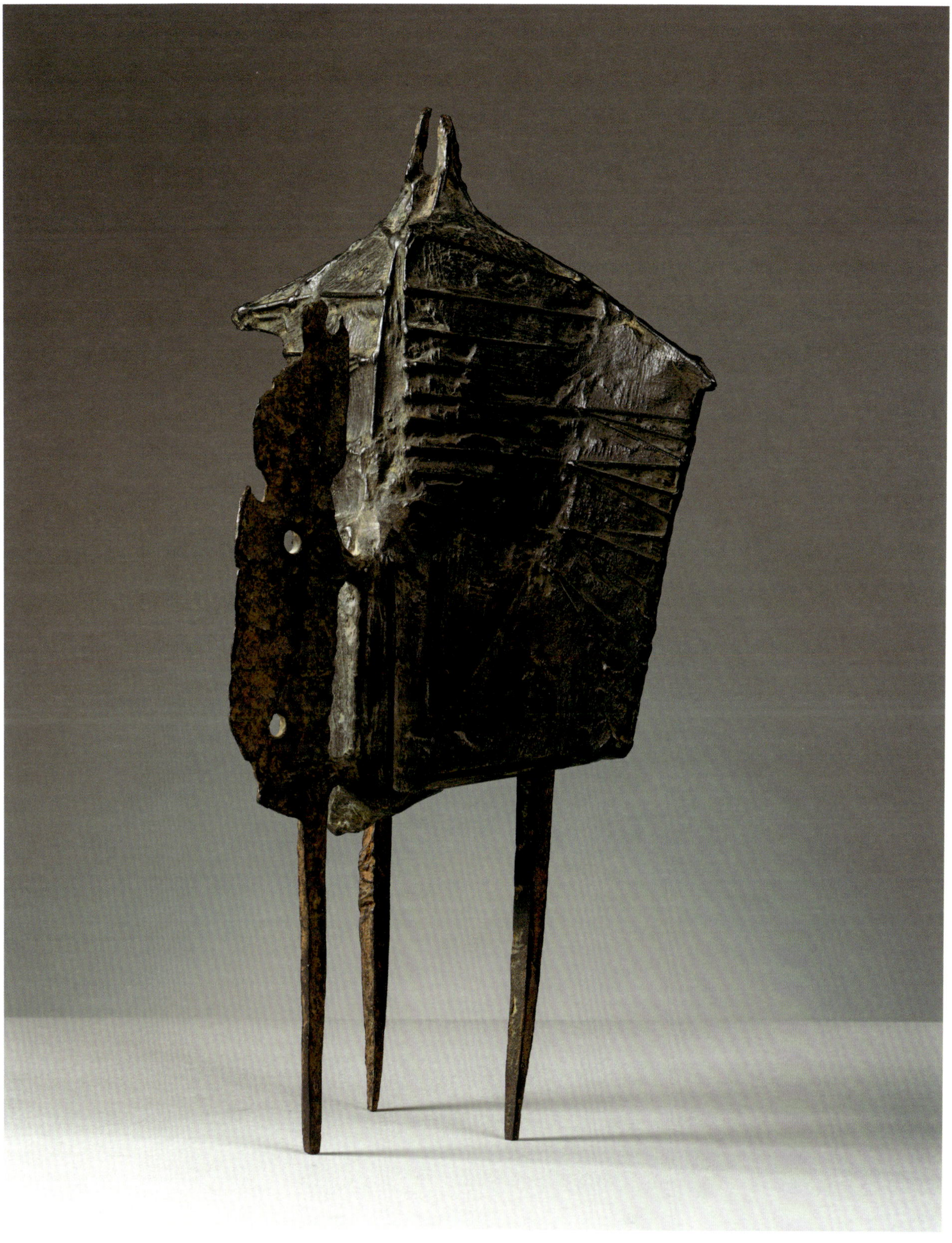

Lynn Chadwick (1914-2003)

Teddy Boy and Girl II, 1957
Bronze
Edition of 4
Cast by Fondeur Susse Freres, Paris 1961
208 x 59 x 52.5 cms (81¾ x 23¼ x 20¾ in)

Provenance
Private Collection (for 50 years)

Exhibited
Marlborough Fine Art, London, November - December 1961

Literature
Lynn Chadwick Sculpture, Dennis Farr & Eva Chadwick, published by Lund Humphries, no.227, p.130
Oberlin College Bulletin, 15/102 (Winter 1958), 69
Les Beaux-Arts, 946-947 (Oct. 1961), 10
Martin H. Bush (introd.), Edwin A. Ulrich Museum of Art (Wichita State University, Wichita, Kansas, 1980), 29

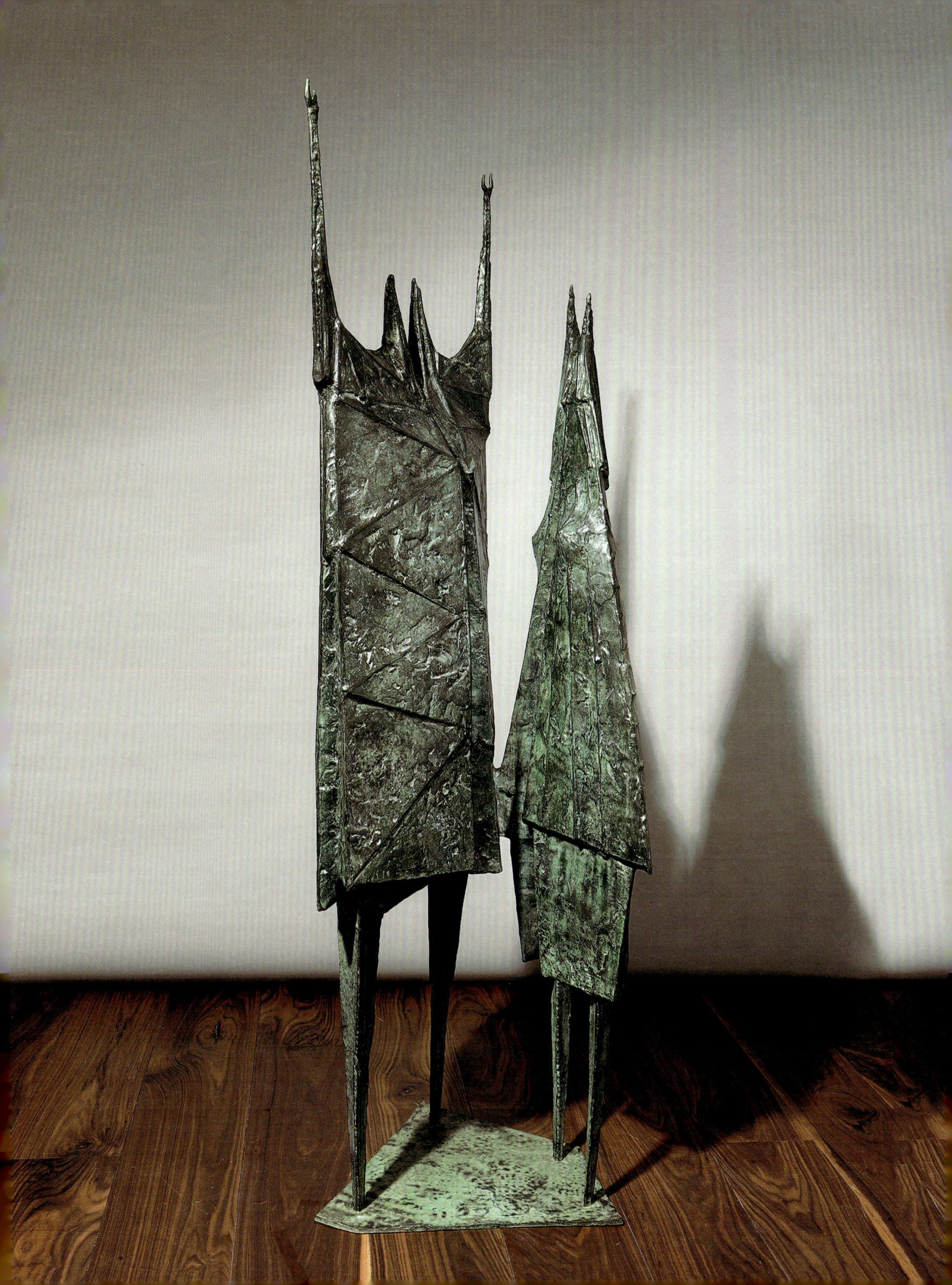

Lynn Chadwick (1914-2003)

Conjunction II, 1957
Bronze
Signed, inscribed and numbered from the edition of 9
Cast at Lypiatt, 1983
84.5 x 51 x 12.5 cms (33¼ x 20 x 5 in)

Provenance
Geert van der Veen, Toronto
Private Collection, Canada, acquired from the above 1979
Private Collection, UK

Literature
Lynn Chadwick Sculptor, Dennis Farr & Eva Chadwick, published by Lund Humphries, no. 220, p.128

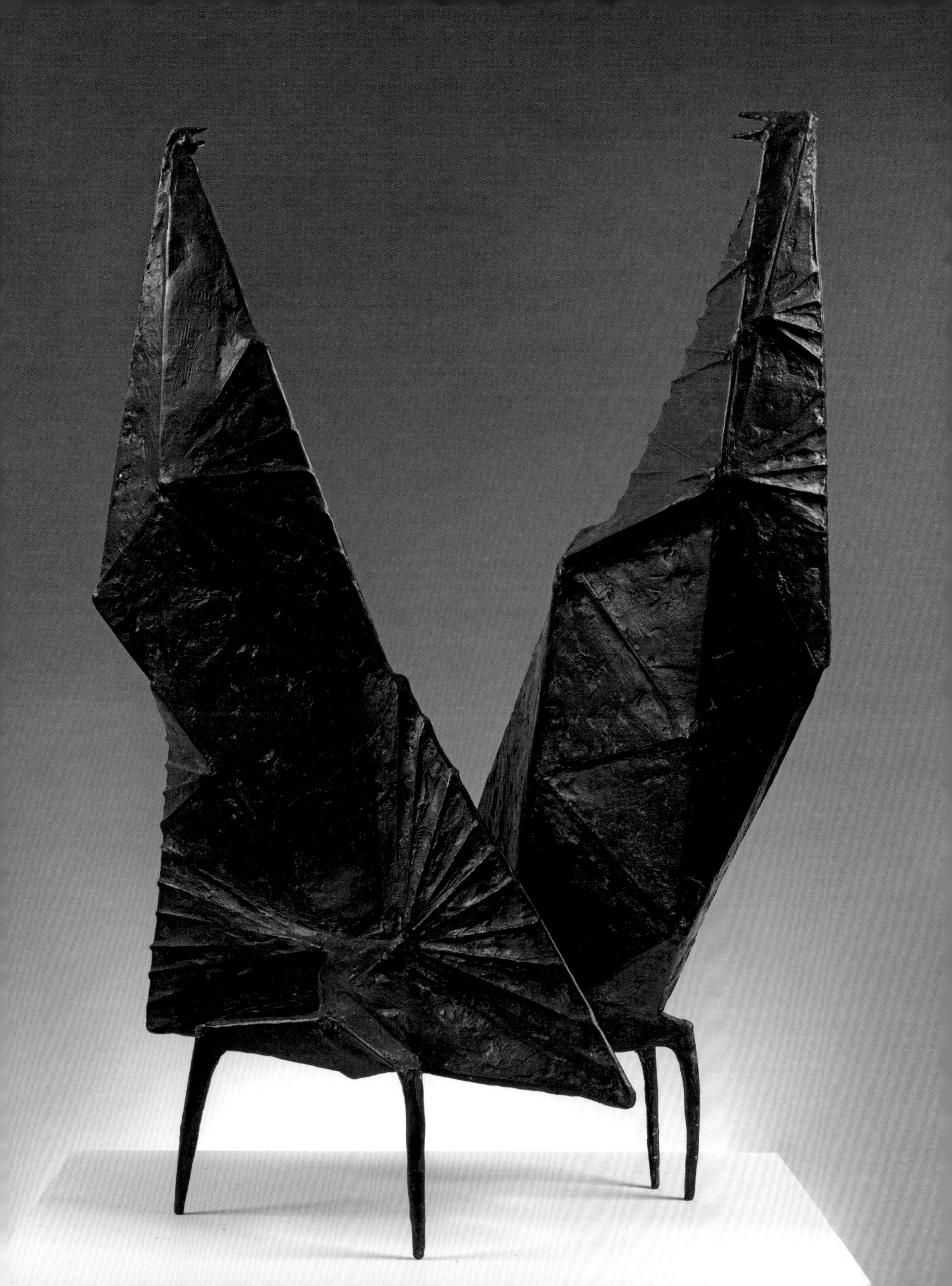

Lynn Chadwick (1914-2003)

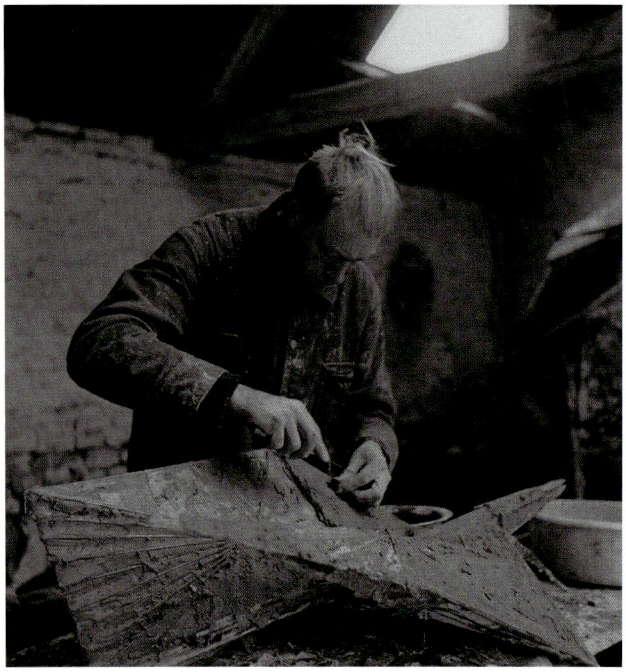

© Photograph by David Farrell

Bird III, 1958
Bronze
Edition of 4
Cast by A&B Foundry in 1961
32 x 122 x 50 cms (12½ x 48 x 19¾ in)

Provenance
Knoedler Galleries, New York
Private Collection, purchased from the above 1961
Private Collection, UK

Exhibited
Lynn Chadwick, Knoedler Galleries, New York, 1961, no.5
Sculpture from the Albert A List Family Collection, New York Art Center, 1965
Birds in Contemporary Art, The Phillips Collection, Washington DC, 1966
Temple Sholom, loan exhibit, Greenwich, CT, USA, 1975

Literature
Lynn Chadwick Sculptor, Dennis Farr & Eva Chadwick, published by Lund Humphries, no. 252, p.132
Motif, 4, March 1960, p.25

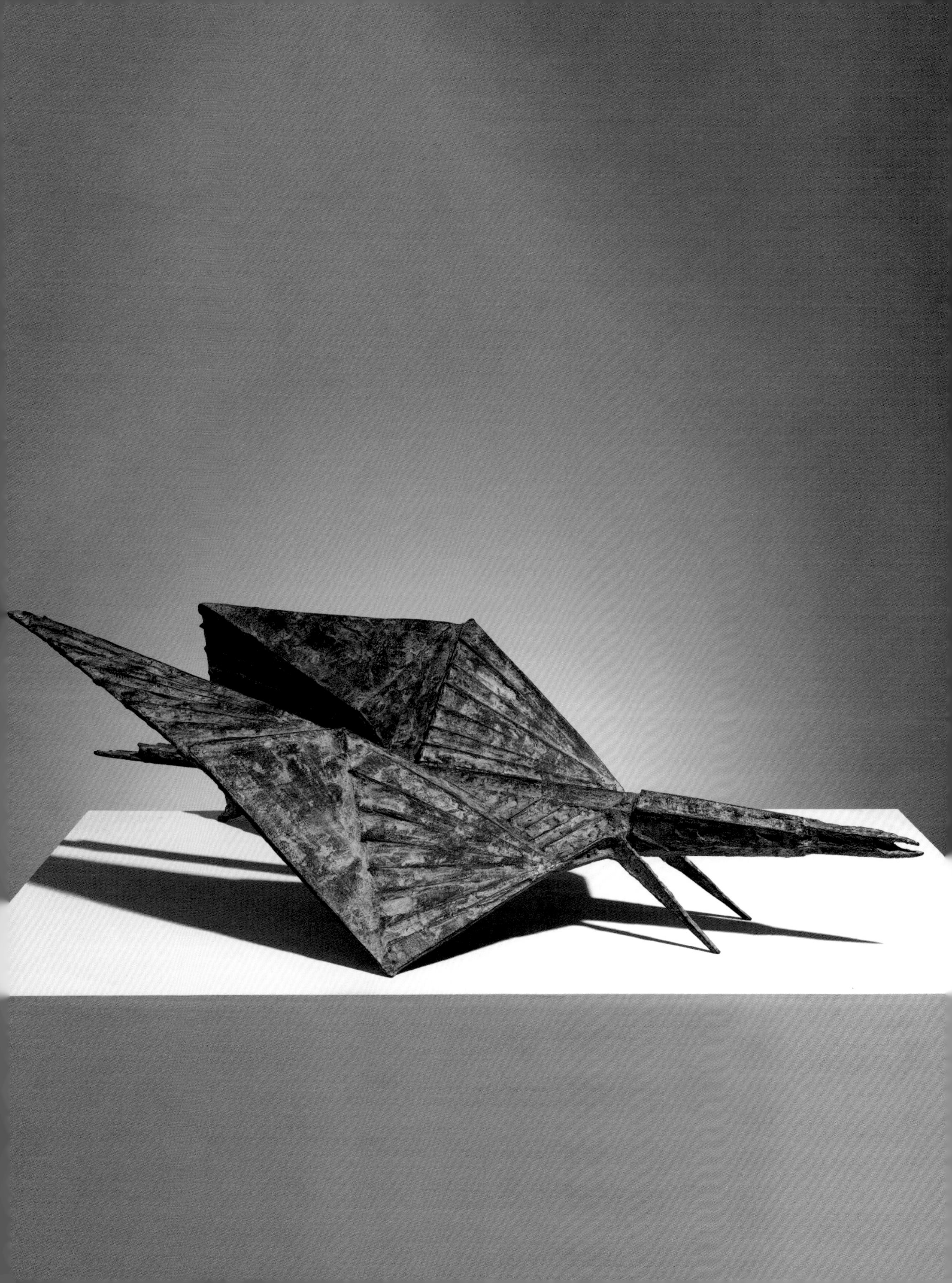

Lynn Chadwick (1914-2003)

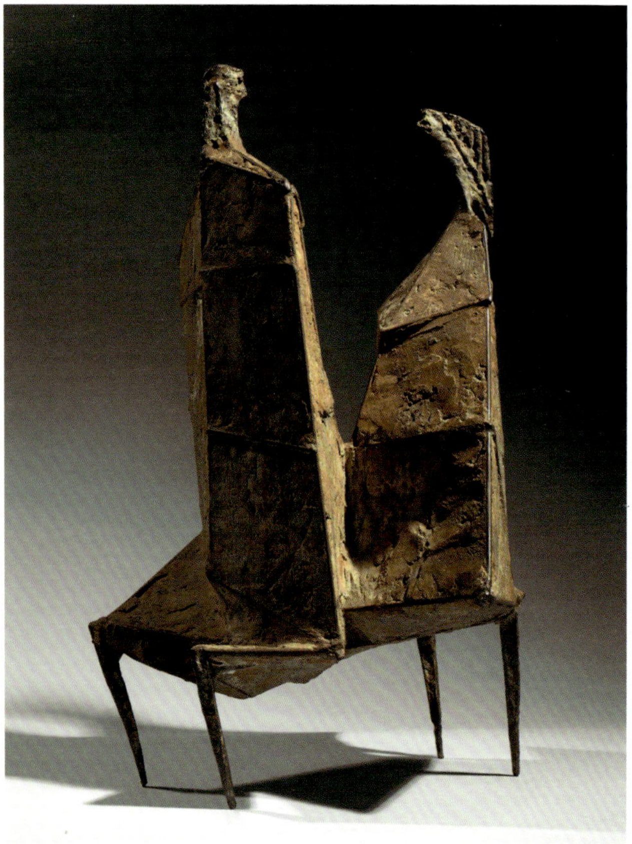

Dance XII, 1958
Iron and composition
Unique
66 x 40 x 38 cms (26 x 15¾ x 15 in)

Provenance
Private Collection, Switzerland

Exhibited
Galerie Daniel Cordier, Paris, May 1958

Literature
Lynn Chadwick Sculpture, Dennis Farr & Eva Chadwick, published by Lund Humphries, no.253, p.133

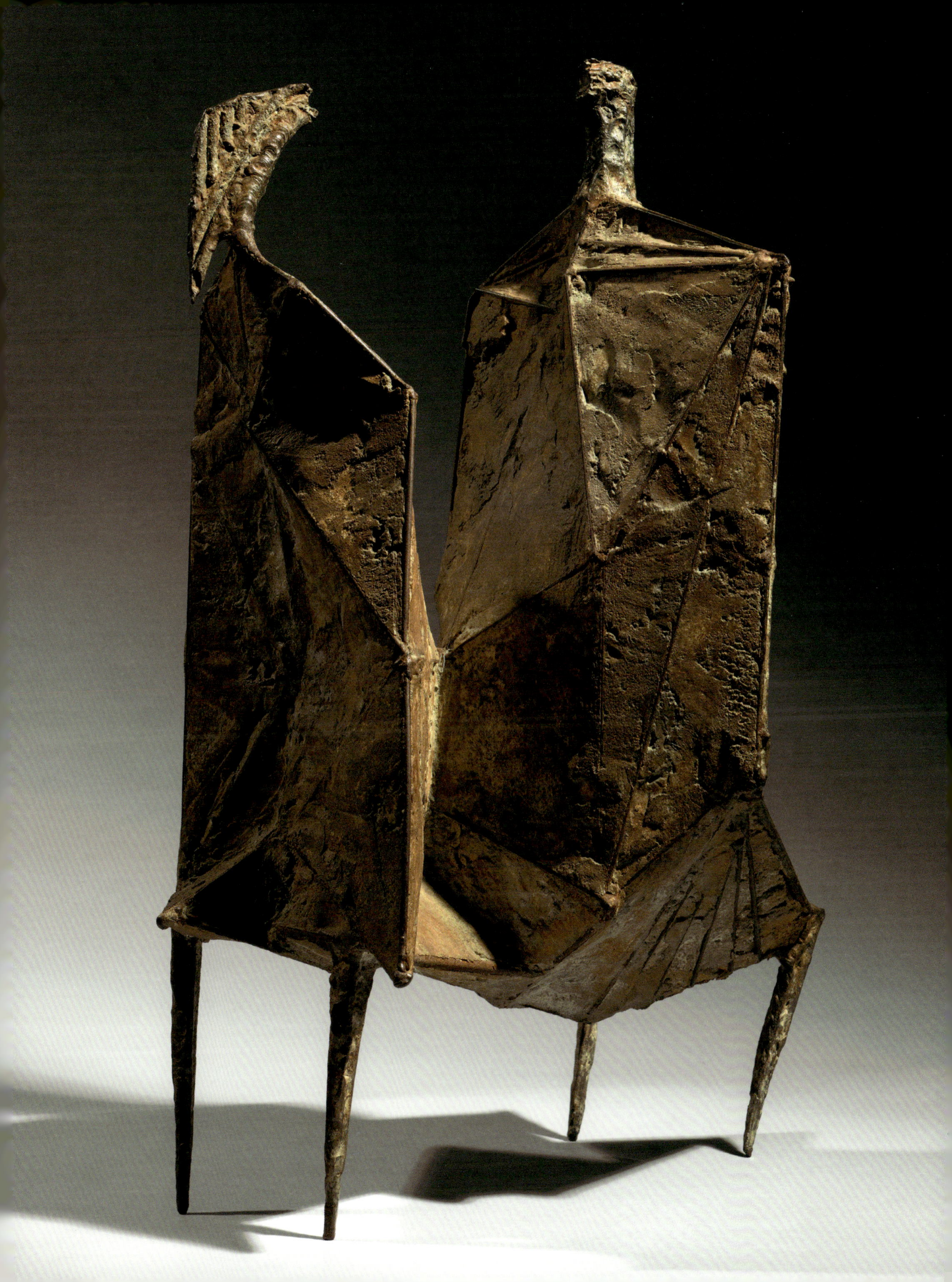

Lynn Chadwick (1914-2003)

Conjunction V, 1958
Bronze
Signed and numbered from the edition of 9
52.4 x 33 x 25 cms (20½ x 13 x 9¾ in)

Literature
Lynn Chadwick Sculptor, Dennis Farr & Eva Chadwick,
published by Lund Humphries, no. 277, p.149

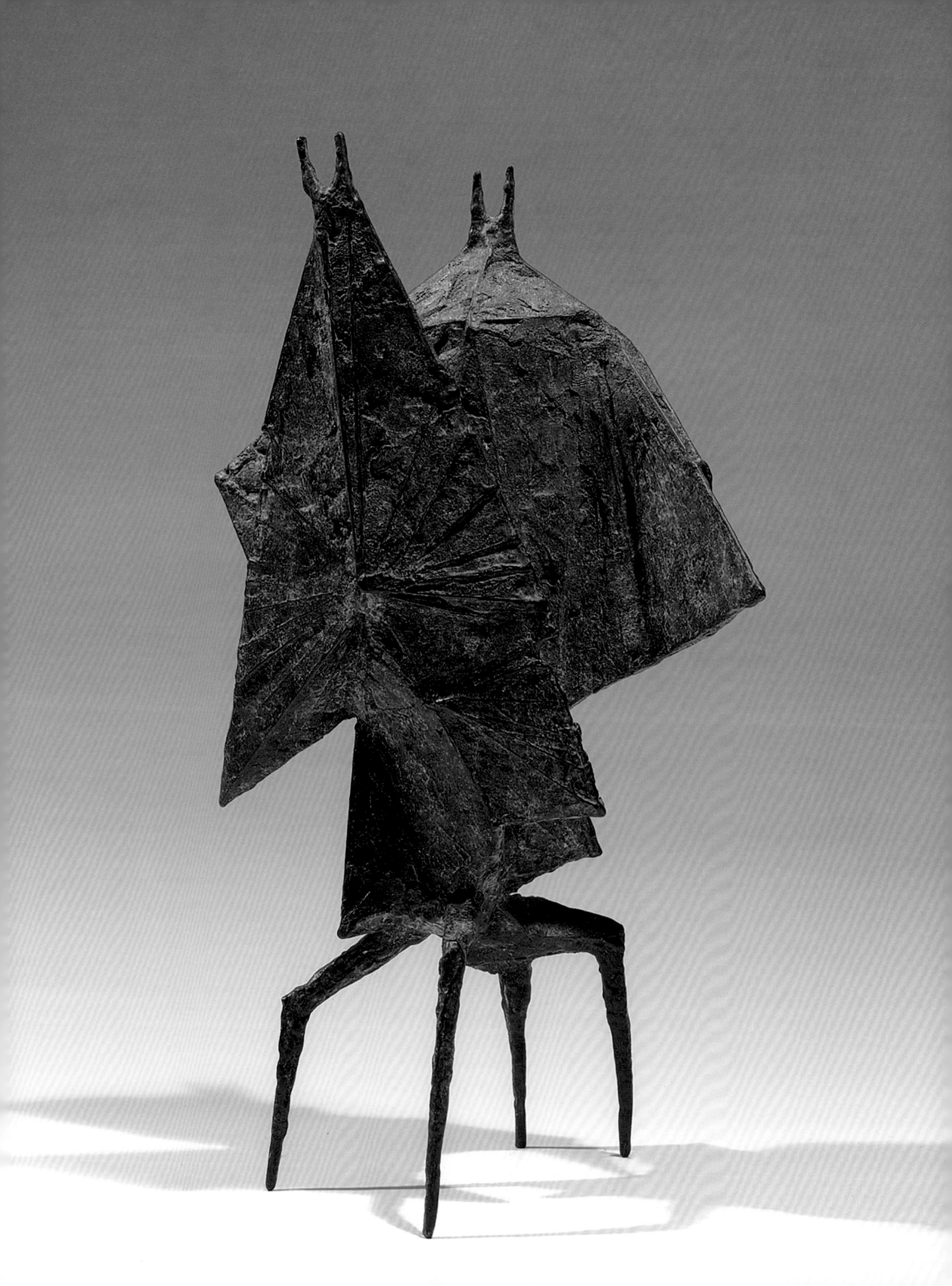

Lynn Chadwick (1914-2003)

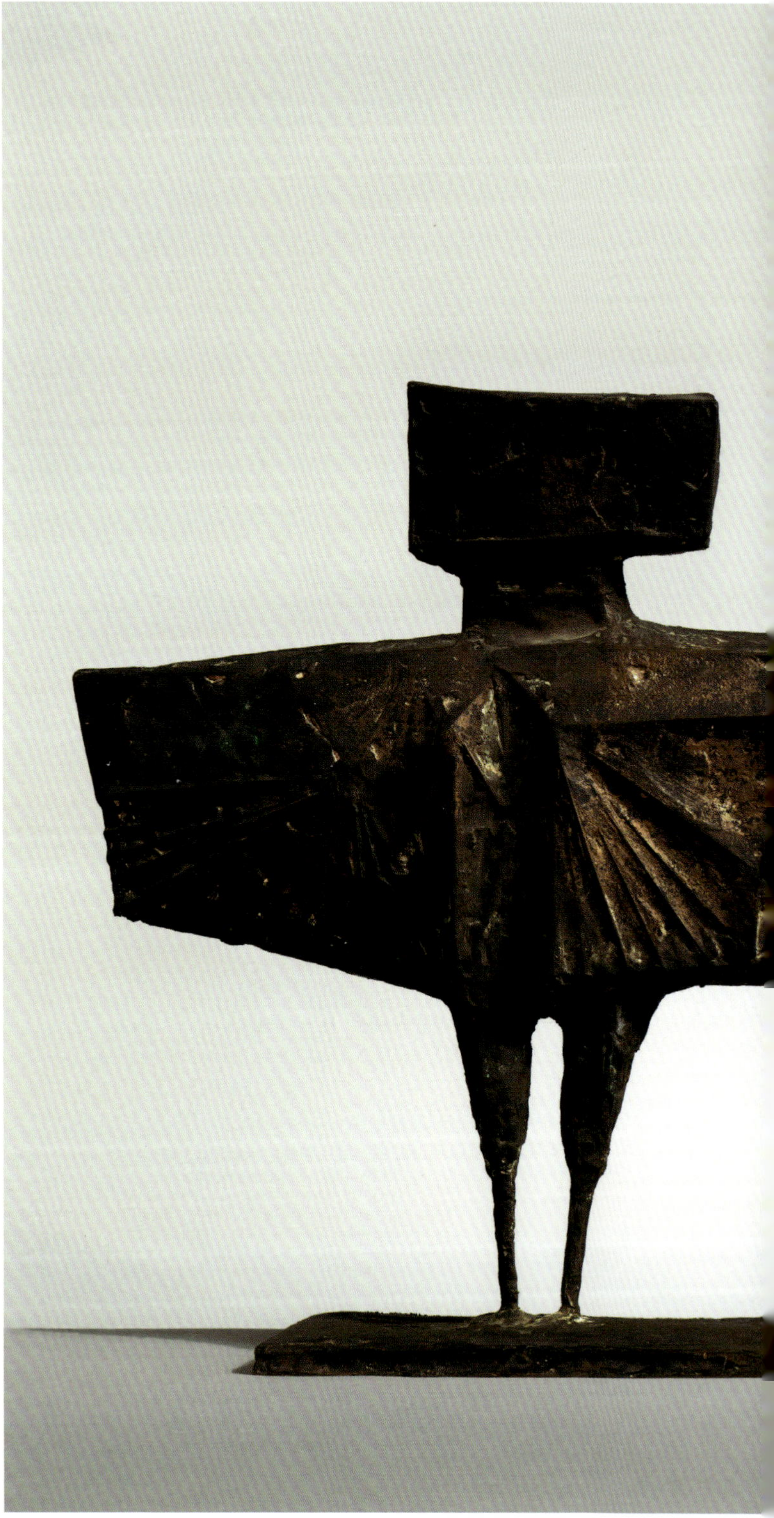

Three Winged Figures, 1960
Bronze
Signed and numbered from the edition of 4
Inscribed with the blindstamp of Brotal foundry, Mendriso, Switzerland
51 x 112 x 17 cms (20 x 44 x 6¾ in)

Exhibited
Marlborough Fine Art, London, Nov. - Dec. 1961 (another cast)

Literature
Lynn Chadwick Sculpture, Dennis Farr & Eva Chadwick, published by Lund Humphries, no.333, p.166

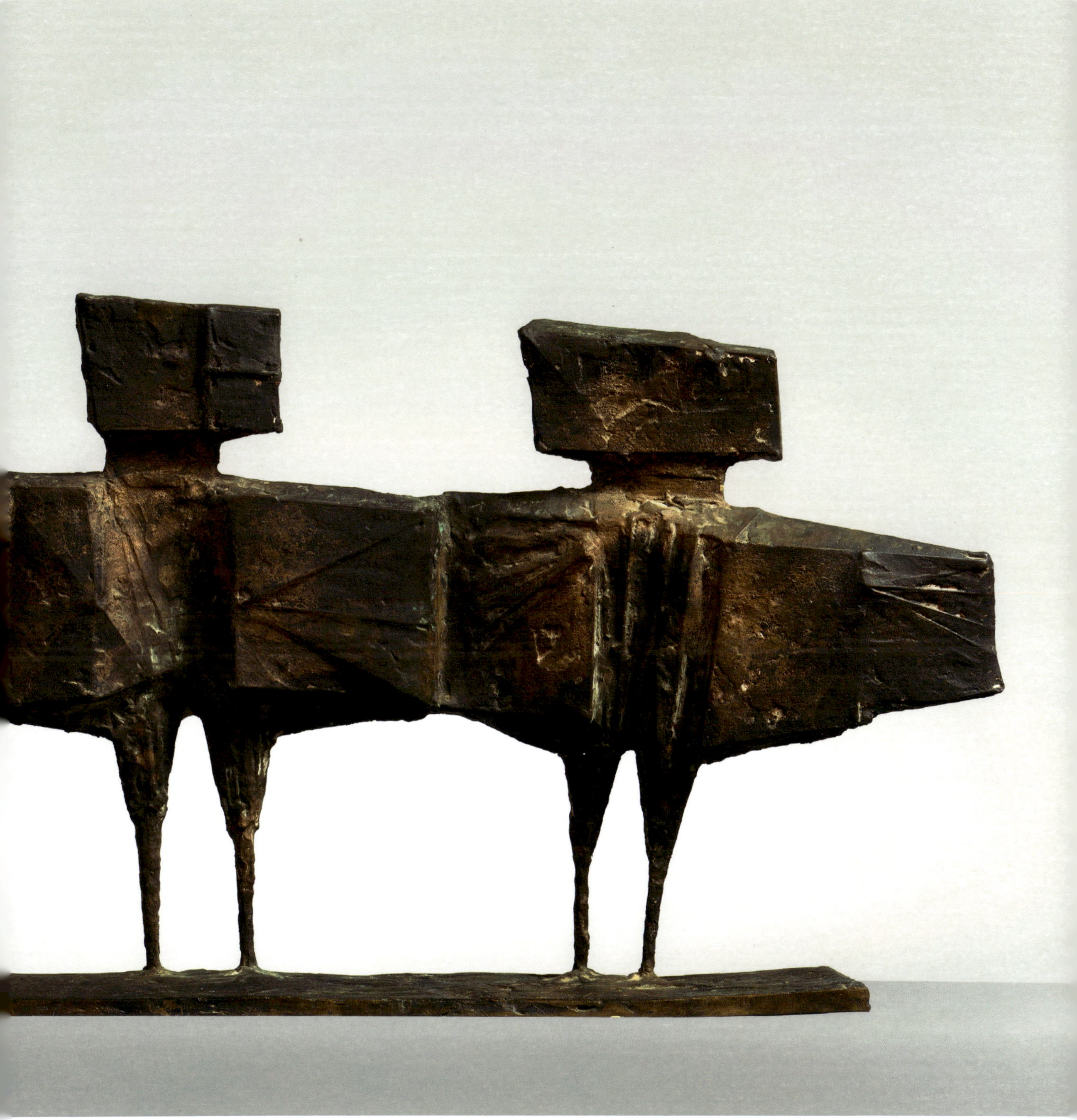

Lynn Chadwick (1914-2003)

Two Winged Figures II, 1976
Bronze
Each figure intitialled and numbered from the edition of 8
Cast in January 1979 by Lypiatt Foundry
49 x 47 x 17 cms (19¼ x 18½ x 6¾ in)

Provenance
Private Collection, Belgium

Exhibited
Galerie Farber, Brussels, Lynn Chadwick, Victor Pasmore,
November - December 1976

Literature
Lynn Chadwick Sculptor, Dennis Farr & Eva Chadwick, published
by Lund Humphries, no. 735, p.320

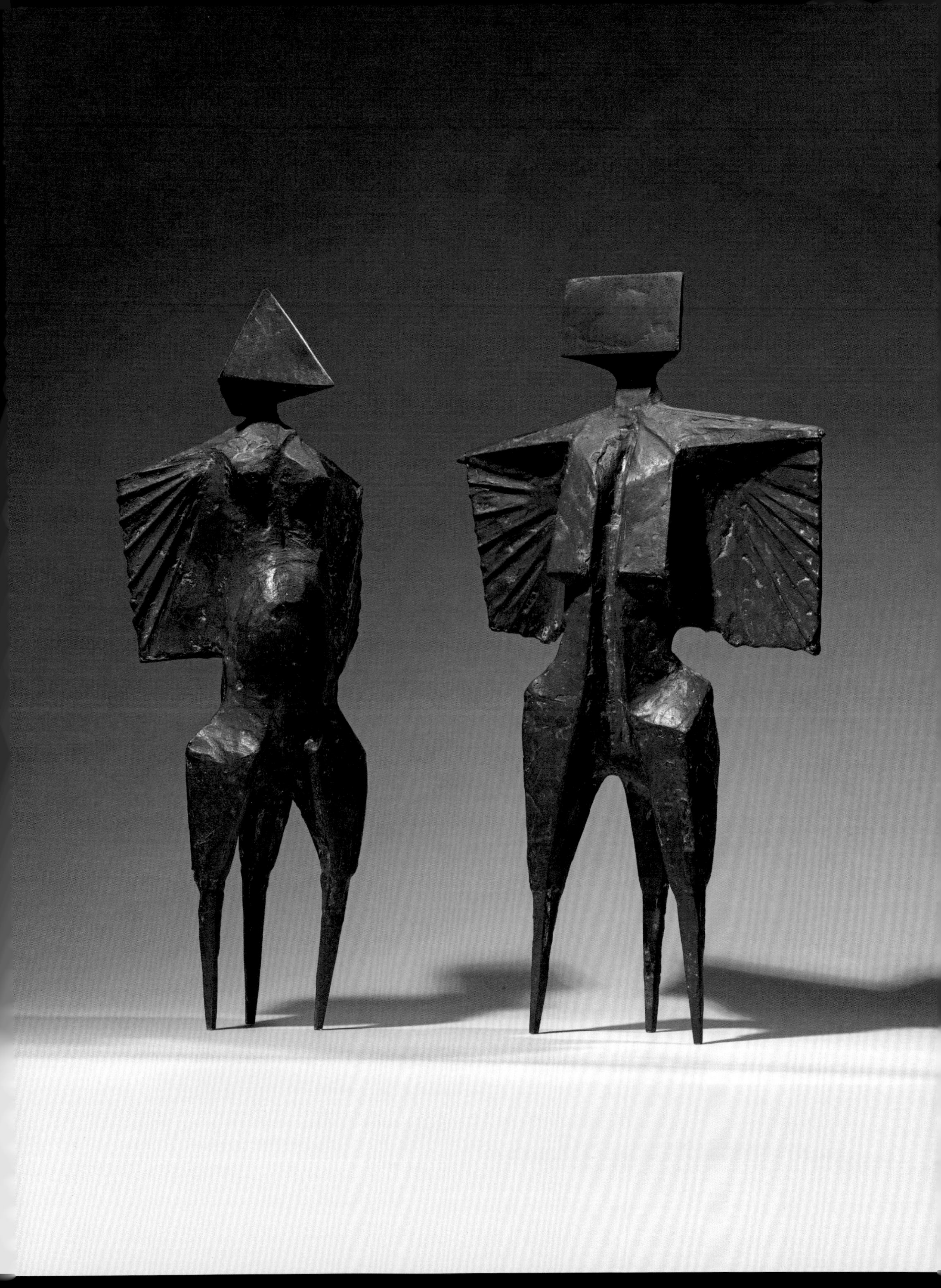

Bernard Meadows (1915-2005)

If Read, in penning the over-quoted paragraph summing up the character of British post-war sculpture, had had a particular artist's work it mind, it was surely Meadows' crab and cockerel sculptures to which he was referring in his second sentence: 'Here are images of flight, of ragged claws 'scuttling across floors of silent seas' ....' And Meadows' career illustrates another characteristic of an admittedly limited number of celebrated British artists' careers in the first twenty-five years or so after the war: that a role in teaching could financially underpin the creative artist's career. This – certainly unintentionally – would lead to so many artists' career illusions that after college simply 'making work in the studio' would be sufficient to provide a living. That was the ethos that so many art colleges imparted, concealing the essential financial cushion that a teaching salary provided. After his 'apprenticeship' with Henry Moore and his war service, Meadows first taught sculpture at Chelsea School of Art and at the Bath Academy from 1948, before becoming Professor of Sculpture at the Royal College of Art from 1960 till retirement in 1980.

As a second-year art student at Norwich, on a group visit to Moore's studio, Meadows so impressed the sculptor that Moore invited the 19-year old to be his assistant (and occasionally to stay at his home in Kent). Meadows would assist him with the carving of the large Hornton stone 'Recumbent Figure' (1939) and the large elm wood 'Reclining Figure' (1939) before going on to complete his studies at the Royal College. After his war service, from 1946 to 1948 he again assisted Moore, particularly on the 'Three Standing Figures' (1948) which was unveiled at the first Open Air Sculpture Exhibition at Battersea Park that year. Moore's biographer, Roger Berthoud has written that Moore's relationship with the young sculptor was to be the master's most enduring by far with another artist, and Moore would also support Meadows' ambition to embark on a teaching career.

Large 'Jesus' Crab, 1952
Bronze
Edition of 6
72 x 75 x 12 cms (28 ¼ x 30 x 4 ¾ in)

Provenance
The Artist, until 1965
Private Collection, UK

Exhibited
The British Pavilion, XXXII Biennale 1964, Venice
Amsterdam, Stedelijk Museum, *Roger Hilton, Gwyther Irwin, Bernard Meadows, Joe Tilson,* 13 May-21 June 1965; this exhibition travelled to Zagreb, Modern Gallery, Berlin, Kunstamt Reinickendorf, Museen der Stadt Recklinghausen and Kunstverein Braunschweig (this cast)

Literature
John Rothenstein, *British Art Since 1900*, Phaidon, London, 1962, pl.145
Alan Bowness, *Bernard Meadows, Sculpture and Drawings*, Lund Humphries, London, 1995, p.138, cat.no.BM28

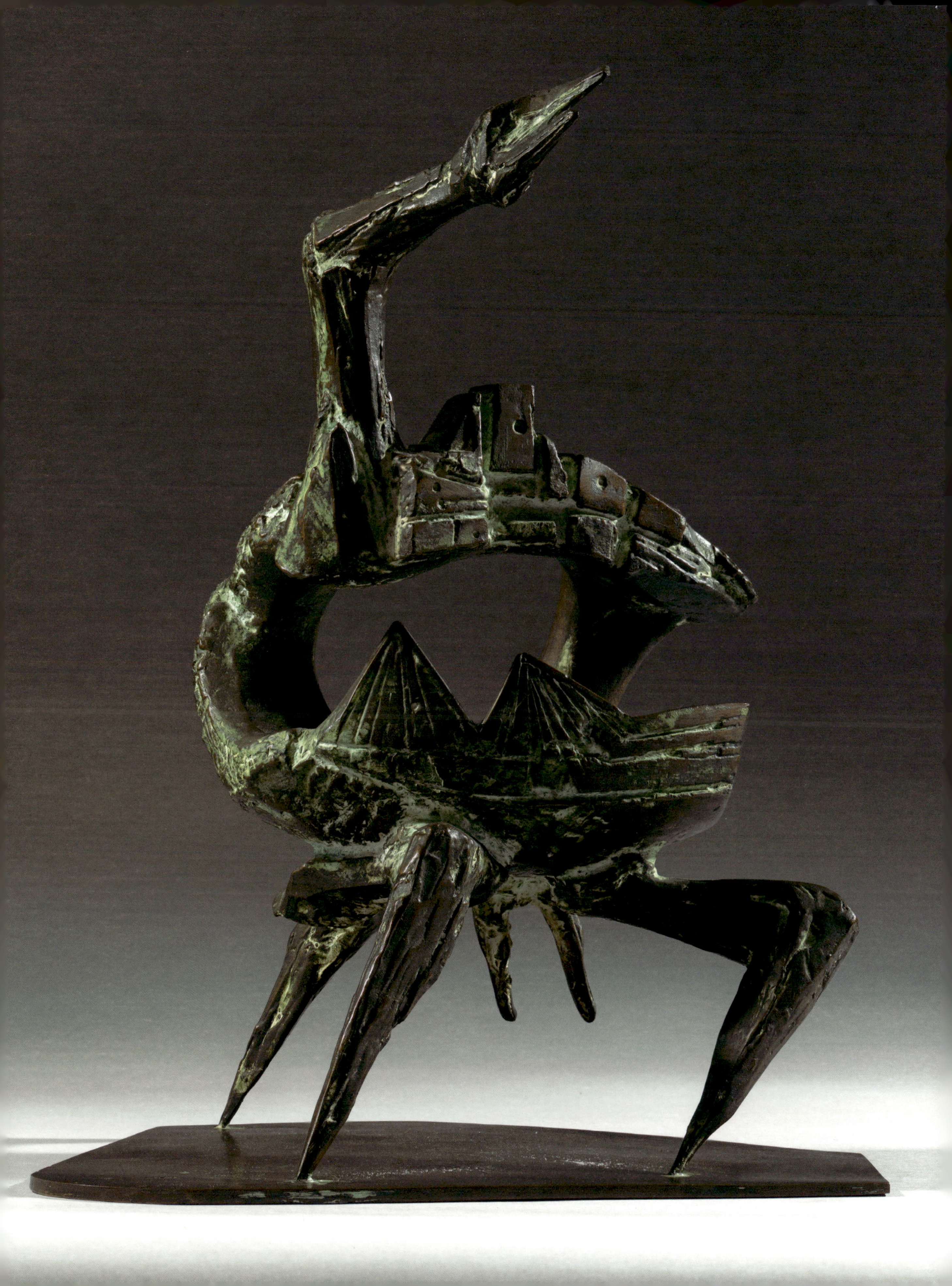

Bernard Meadows (1915-2005)

He had initiated the young Meadows into Surrealism, when both contributed work to the 1936 International Surrealist Exhibition at the New Burlington Galleries. This orientation would play a role in Meadows' later choice of animal subjects as surrogates for his life-long left-leaning views on human nature and the structures of power, aggression and exploitation – no doubt reinforced by the strongly contrasted values of combatants in the World War in which he also played his part. Posted at one stage in the war to the Cocos and Comoros Islands in the Indian Ocean, Meadows had some leisure to observe the behaviour of its wildlife; birds, snakes, spiders and particularly the large variety of crabs that populated the islands' shores. His interest in settling on animal subjects for sculpture had earlier been stimulated by Picasso's unorthodox 'Cockerel' (1932) in particular, which theme the Spaniard would occasionally revisit in sculpture during and after the war, with 'Cat', 'Man and Sheep', 'Crane', 'Little Owl' and 'Goat'.

After his earliest post-war sculptures of standing figures – in part his homage to Moore – Meadows produced an over-life size 'Cockerel' in bronze for a schools commission in 1950, and started his series of crabs and birds in the following year, which would occupy him for the next decade.

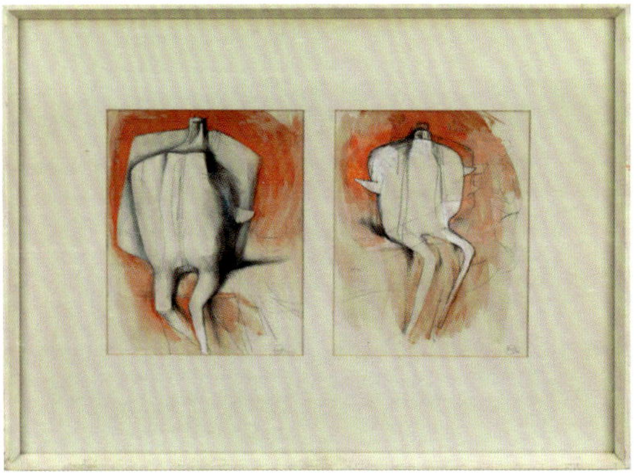

Left:
Drawing for Sculpture (Two Seated Figures), 1962
Gouache
Initialled and dated on each sheet lower right
Each 26.5 x 20 .5 cms (10 ½ x 8 in)

Provenance
Private Collection, UK

Exhibited
The British Pavilion, XXXII Biennale 1964, Venice

Seated Armed Figure, 1962
Bronze
Edition of 6
44.5 x 45 x 26 cms (17½ x 17¾ x 10¼ in)

Provenance
Gimpel fils, London
Private Collection, USA, purchased from the above, 1964

Literature
Bernard Meadows, Sculpture and Drawings, Alan Bowness, published by The Henry Moore Foundation is association with Lund Humphries, 1995, no, BM81, p.143

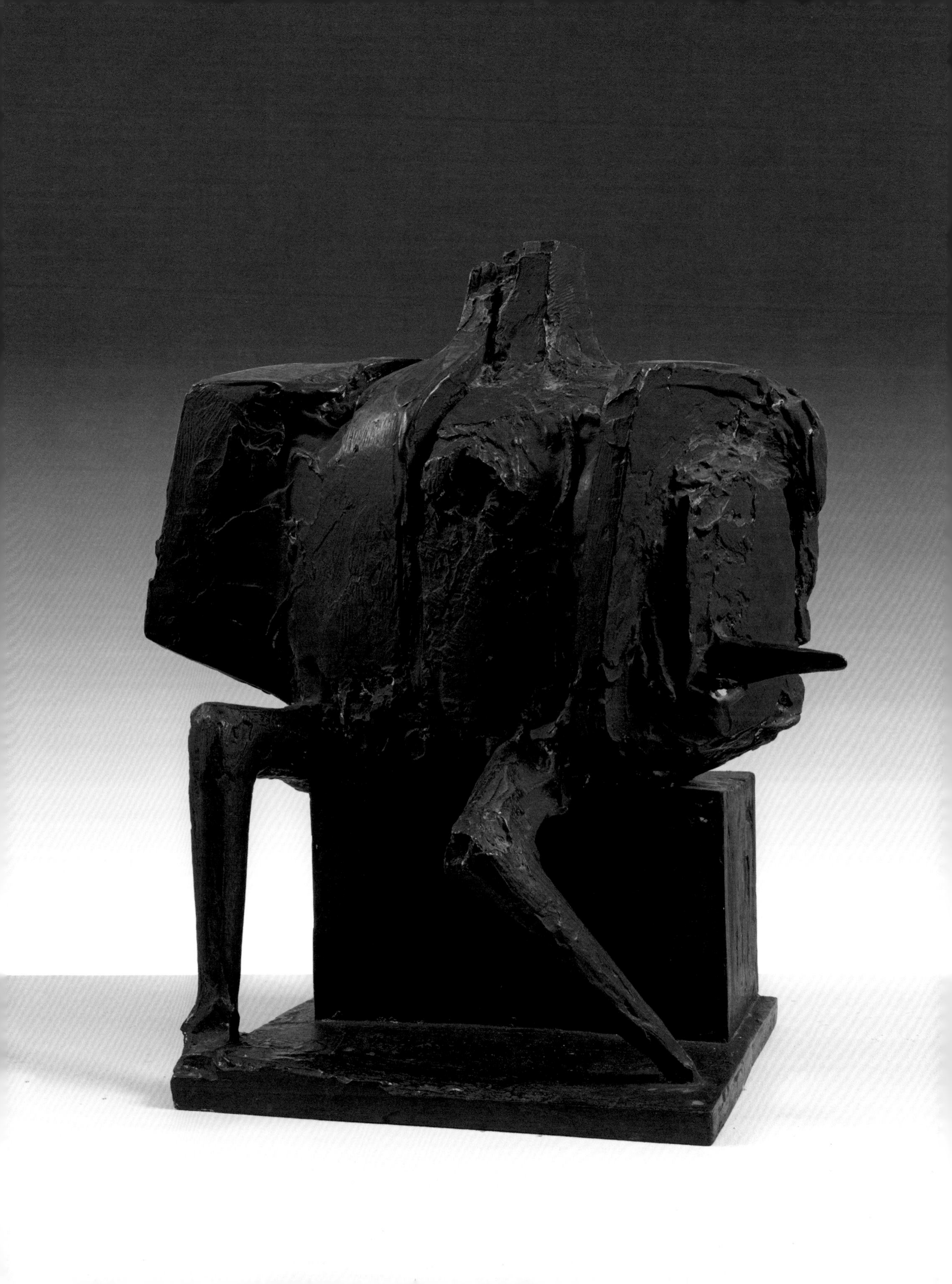

Bernard Meadows (1915-2005)

He was well aware of the 'difficulty' of these subjects, but he admitted to not wishing to produce merely 'pleasing work'. Shortly after 1960 he embarked on a new 'awkward' subject, which he designated alternately as 'Armed Figures', 'Directors' or 'Tycoons'. Indeed, these were far from pleasing or attractive: fat block-like figures with tiny heads and spindly, dangling legs. To see a parallel with crabs would not be amiss.

The change had been provoked by the encounter, on a visit to Italy, with a full length Renaissance seated sculpture of a ruthless condottiere, and in particular with Michelangelo's bust of Brutus in the Bargello in Florence. Michelangelo had abandoned the unfinished sculpture, because he felt him to be, in his own words, 'a beast in human form'. The characteristics shared between crab and armed figures (and directors and tycoons) was clear to Meadows: both were protected by armour on the outside, sheltering a soft and vulnerable anatomy inside. Contemporary tycoons, he wrote '...are protected by the paraphernalia of their offices and retinues, but [they] are soft inside. Bullies are frightened people'. How contemporary is that?

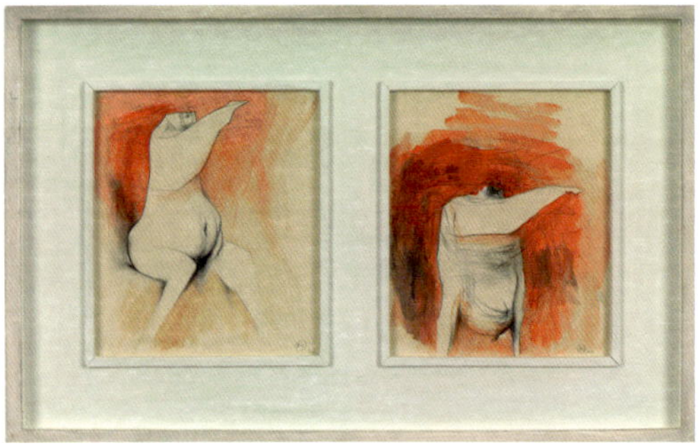

Study for The Two Directors
Gouache
Initialled and dated on each sheet lower right
26.5 x 21 cms (10 ½ x 8 ¼ in)

Provenance
Private Collection, UK

Two Directors, 1963
Two bronze reliefs
Edition of 6
72 x 75 x 12 cms (28¼ x 29½ x 4¾ in)

Provenance
Gimpel fils Gallery, London
Private Collection, USA, purchased from the above in 1964

Exhibited
The British Pavilion, XXXII Biennale Venice, 1964

Literature
Bernard Meadows, Sculpture and Drawings, Alan Bowness, published by The Henry Moore Foundation in association with Lund Humphries, 1995, no, BM93, p.79 & 142

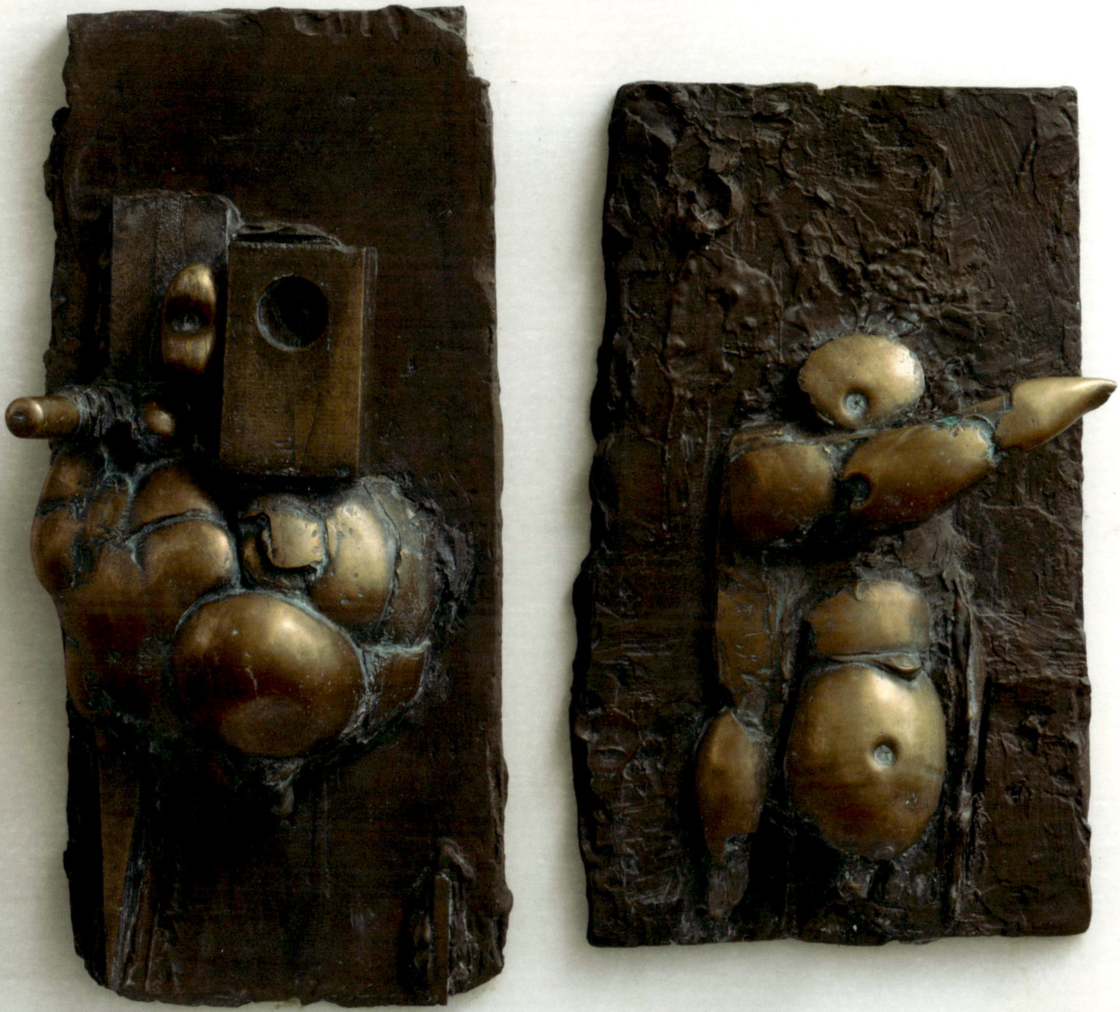

Kenneth Armitage (1916-2002)

As Head of Sculpture at the decidedly non-metropolitan Bath Academy of Art at Corsham between 1946 and 1956, Armitage presents perhaps the antithesis to Meadows in style and subject matter. His work least resembles the tenor of Read's grim characterisation of his generation, as it abounds in a certain tongue-in-cheek humour, and uninhibitedly makes subtle references to the work of some other twentieth century artists. At the end of the 1950's Roland Penrose came to the conclusion that 'a generous warmth in his feeling for humanity distinguishes Armitage from the trend common to many artists of our time who are preoccupied with a sense of anxiety and whose work betrays a feeling of disintegration or aggression'.

Like Adams and Butler, Armitage had studied at art colleges before the war, initially painting before setting out on the path of Moore-inspired carving and experimentation with bronze casting, before the war intervened. He taught tank and aircraft recognition during his war service, and the method of playing with flat silhouettes in the training exercises would translate, more subconsciously than consciously, into the sculpture than he began after the war. That method, which he clearly preferred, involved modelling in plaster on an iron armature, from which he could extend his abbreviated suggestions for heads and limbs.

Family Going for a Walk (Small Version 1), 1950
Bronze
Five casts recorded in the artist's notebook, and annotated as
no. 9 in the artist's archives
(Butler recorded that all casts were sold in the USA)
Cast by Galizia
27.5 x 26 x 14 cms (10¾ x 10¼ x 5½ in)

Provenance
Private Collection, UK

Exhibited
Galerie de France with Gimpel fils, 1952

Literature
The Sculpture of Kenneth Armitage, edited by James Scott, published by Lund Humphries, 2016, no. 10, p.92 (illustration incorrectly substituted for Small Version 2)

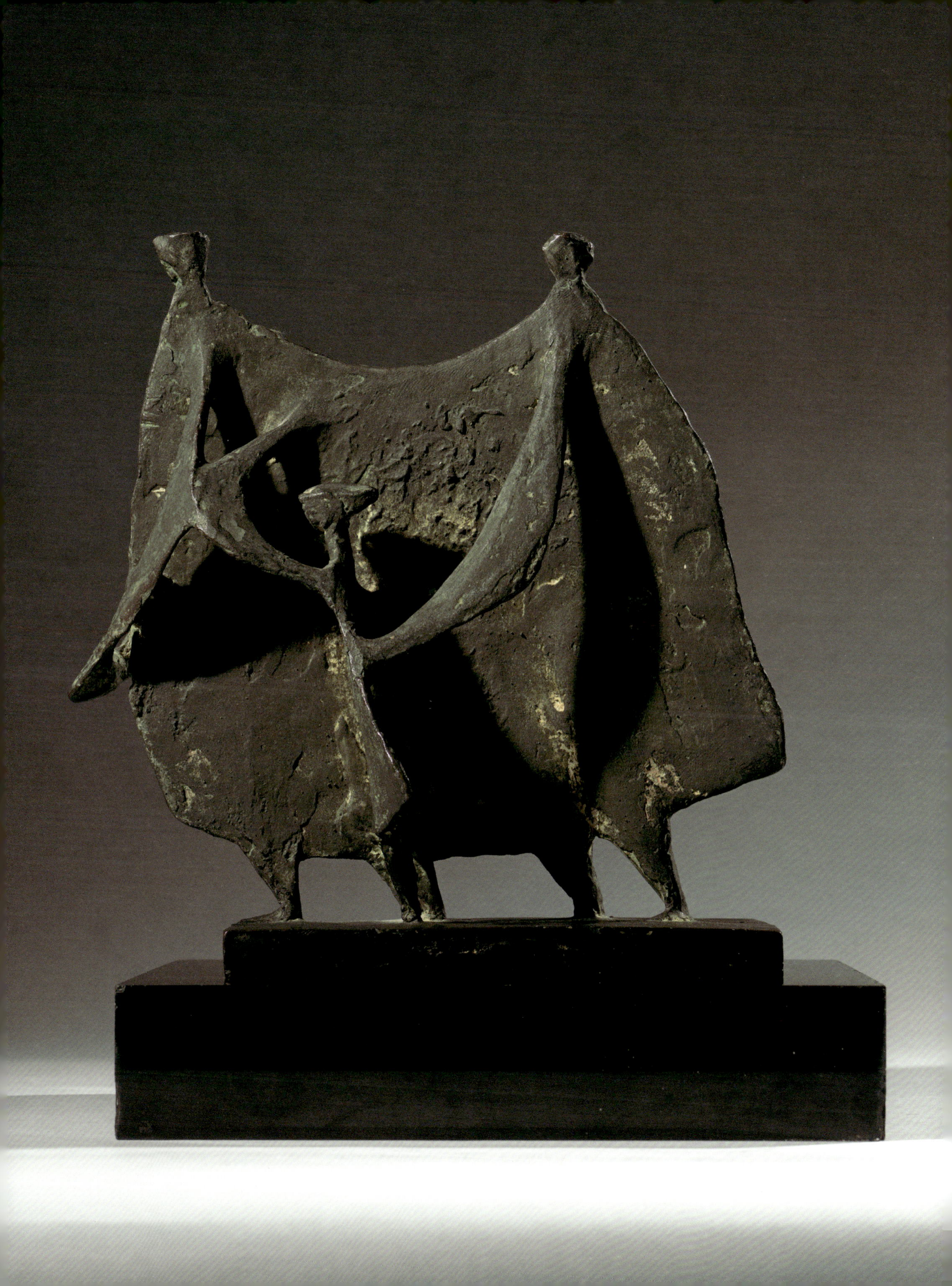

Kenneth Armitage (1916-2002)

Rejecting the all-roundness of Moore and Hepworth, his abstracted figure sculptures appear to emerge out of a screen or a wall. The pin-heads and stubby limbs of 'Family going for a Walk' may draw on Picasso-esque distortions, but the sloping movement of the family is closer to the wit of Klee's drawings. Armitage explained the attraction for him of joining the figures of the family together: 'Two or three figures would be unified into one mass, and then I could arrange the arms and legs as I wanted, because if you look at a crowd, you do not count the arms and legs, you just see odd arms swinging and the odd leg moving. So I could use the arms as I wanted in the design of the maquette'.

In similar vein, the emaciated form of 'Standing Figure' obviously bears some resemblance to Giacometti's post-war bronzes, but the schematic head and bulbous abdomen have a touch of the cheeky paintings of his contemporary Roger Hilton. Indeed the spirit of Hilton's quasi-childlike abstractions can also be seen in other pieces such as the agglomeration of figures in 'The Seasons', and his exaggerated disfiguration of the Moore-like 'Seated Woman with Square Head'. Effectively, Armitage's drawings and gouaches, too, share the deliberate shorthand of the gruff, often interrupted graphic jottings and random patches of colour that typify Hiltons' rapid, energetic écriture.

These are not derivative works, as they all bear his unmistakeable character of brevity to convey the sensation of movement or stasis. They are also recognizably his in the relative flatness and frontality of each group of figures, and show how intelligently Armitage analysed the work of others such as Chadwick or the French sculptor César (in 'Two Seated Figures') or Klee, mentioned above, to create his own gently humorous vision of humankind.

Standing Figure, 1954
Bronze
Edition of 6
80.5 x 19 x 12 cms (31¾ x 7½ x 4¾ in)

Provenance
Parke Bernet, New York
Purchased from the above in 1967 and thence by descent
Private Collection, UK

Literature
Kenneth Armitage: Life and Work, Henry Moore Foundation and Lund Humphries, London (1997), KA50
The Sculpture of Kenneth Armitage, edited by James Scott, published by Lund Humphries, 2016, no. 50, p.103

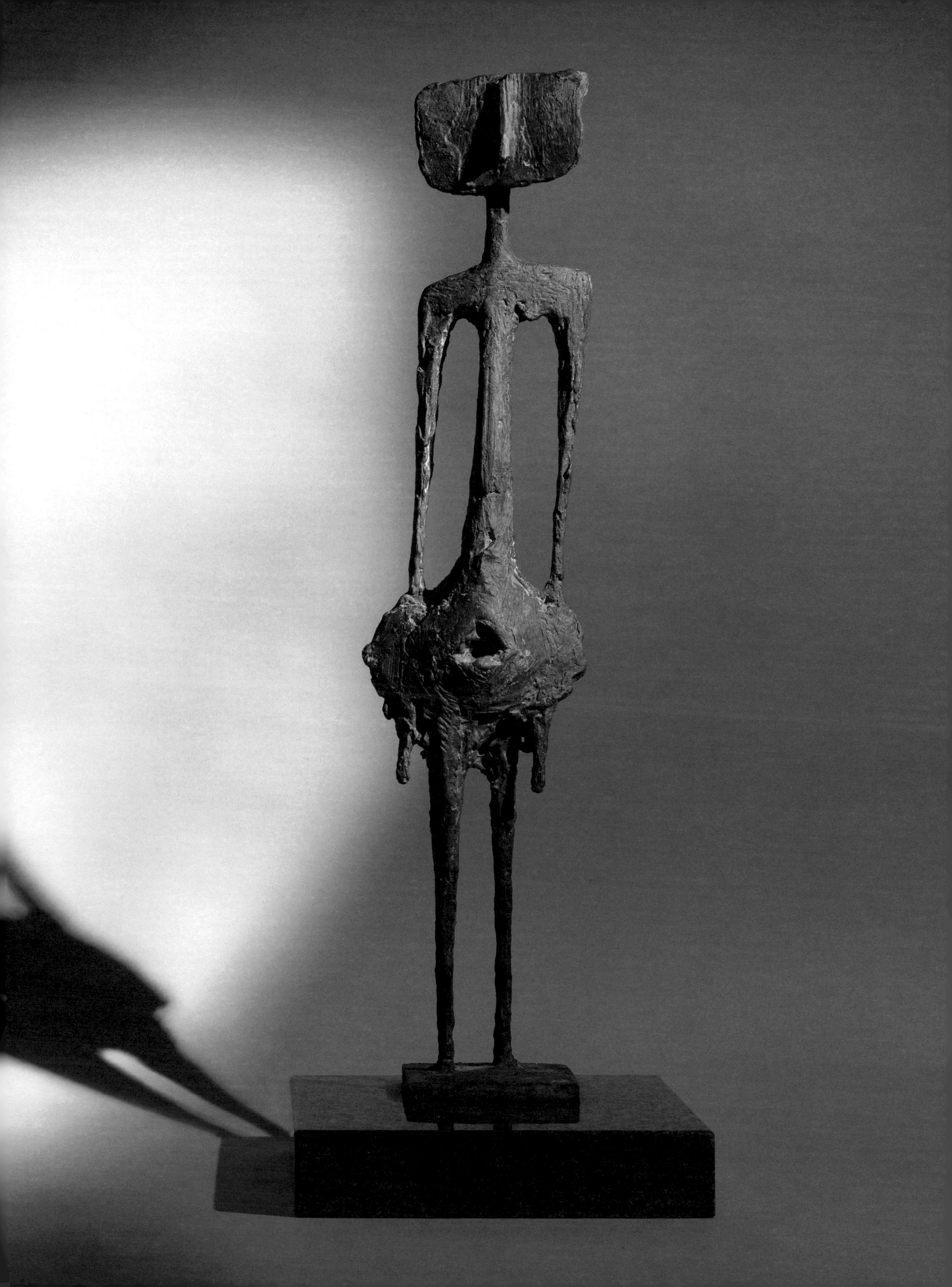

Kenneth Armitage (1916-2002)

Seated Woman with Square Head, 1955
Bronze
Conceived 1955
Cast in 1984 in an edition of 6 casts
Marked with artist's initials and the Susse Freres Foundry mark
61 x 26 x 31 cms (24 x 10¼ x 12¼ in)

Provenance
Private Collection, USA

Exhibited
The British Pavilion, XXIX Biennale, Venice, 1958, cat no 71 (loaned by the Victoria and Albert Museum, London)

Literature
Kenneth Armitage: Life and Work, edited by Alan Bowness, published by Lund Humphries, 1997, p46 , KA54
Norbert Lynton, *Kenneth Armitage*, (London : Methuen, 1962) ill. b/w
Norbert Lynton, *Kenneth Armitage: Art in Progress series* (London : Methuen, 1962) Toby Treves, *British Art in Focus: Patrons' Papers*, (London : Tate, 2004)

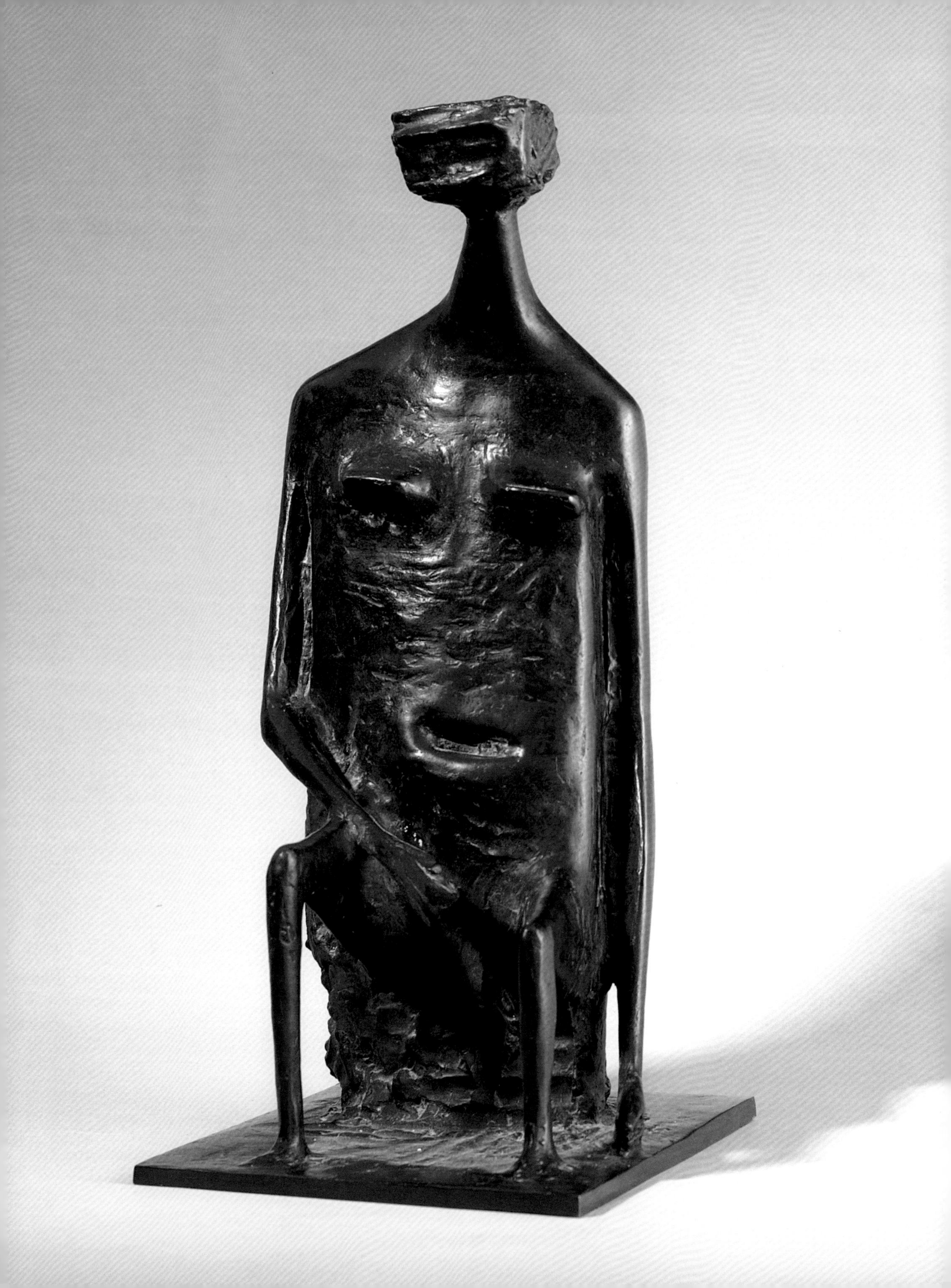

Kenneth Armitage (1916-2002)

Two Standing Figures, 1955
Bronze
Initialled `KA', dated and numbered from the edition of 6
52.5 x 19.5 x 17.0 cms (20¾ x 7¾ x 6¾ in)

Provenance
Private Collection, UK
Gimpel fils, London
Ken Powell
Hazlitt Holland Hibbert
Private Collection, UK

Exhibited
London, Whitechapel Art Gallery, Kenneth Armitage, July - August 1959, cat no.22, another cast, entitled Two Standing Figures

Literature
Kenneth Armitage, by Norbert Lynton, Methuen Art in Progress Series, 1962, p.10
Artists and Patrons in Post-War Britain, edited by Margaret Garlake, published by Ashgate, 2001, p.66-7
The Sculpture of Kenneth Armitage, edited by James Scott, published by Lund Humphries, 2016, no. 56, p.106

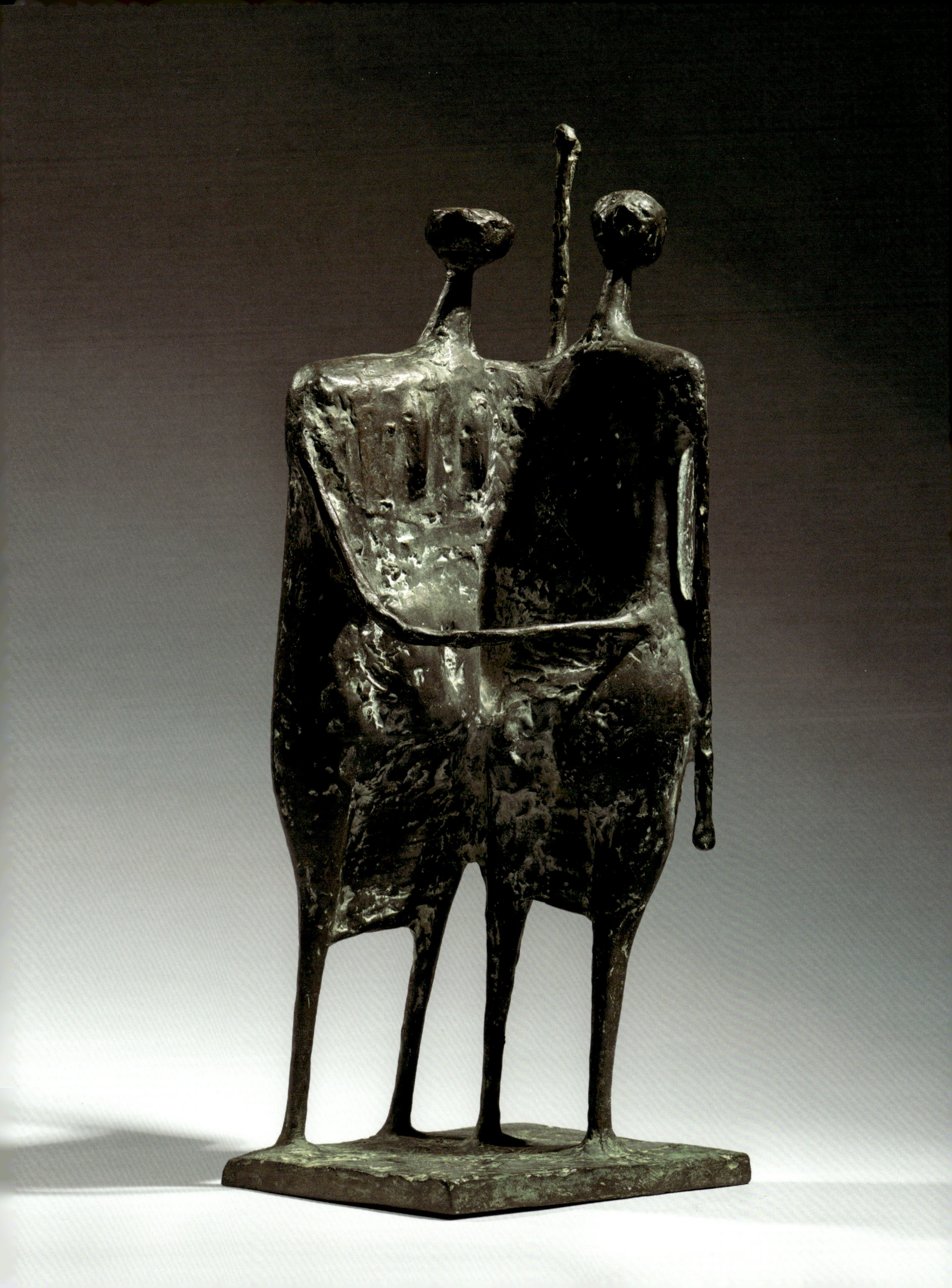

Kenneth Armitage (1916-2002)

The Seasons (Model A), 1956
Bronze
Initialled `KA'
Conceived in 1956, cast in 1987
Artist's cast after the edition of 6
70 x 41 x 28 cms (27½ x 16 x 11 in)

Provenance
Private Collection, South Africa
Private Collection, UK

Literature
The Sculpture of Kenneth Armitage, edited by James Scott, published by Lund Humphries, 2016, no. 65A, p.109

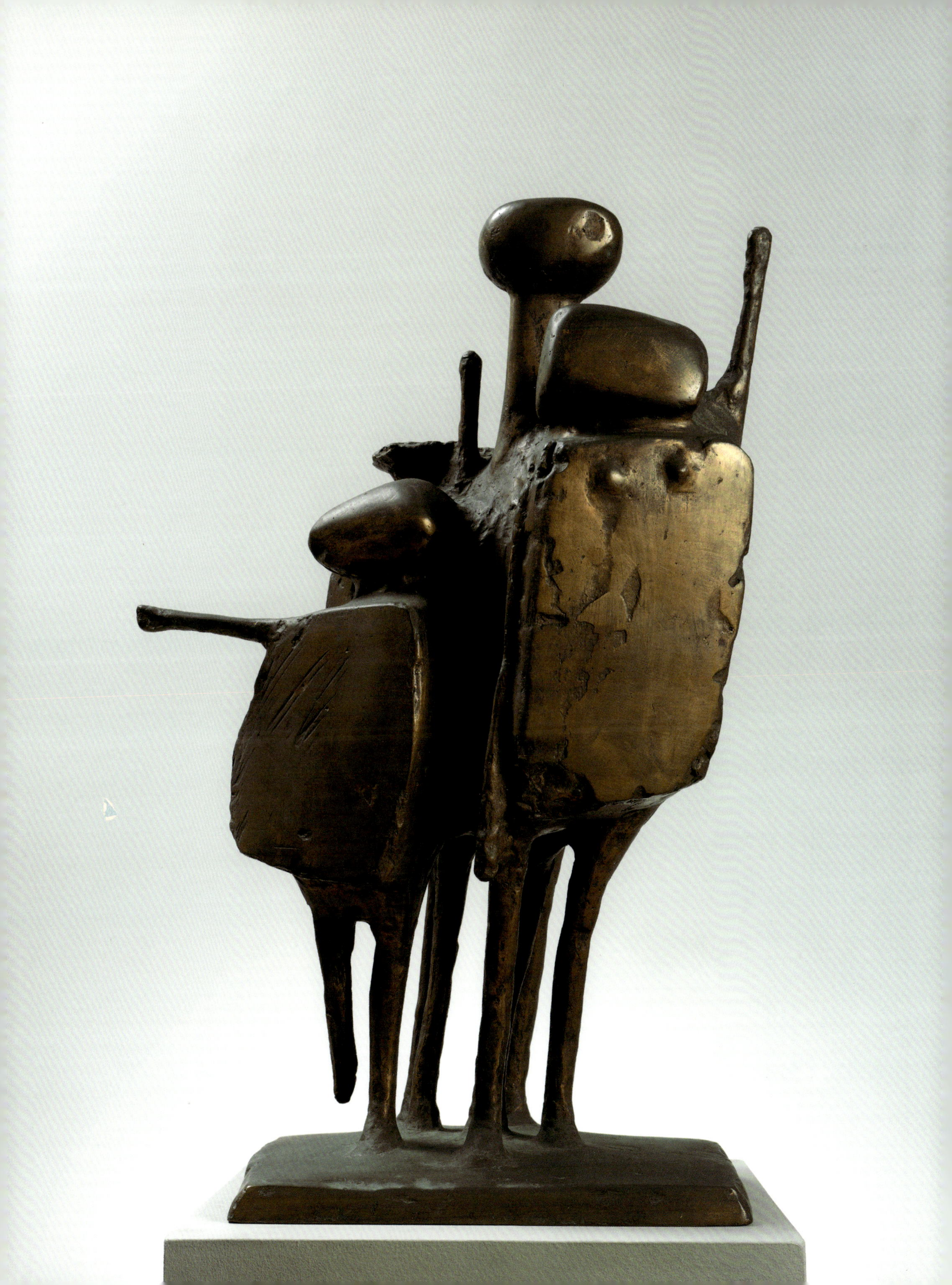

Kenneth Armitage (1916-2002)

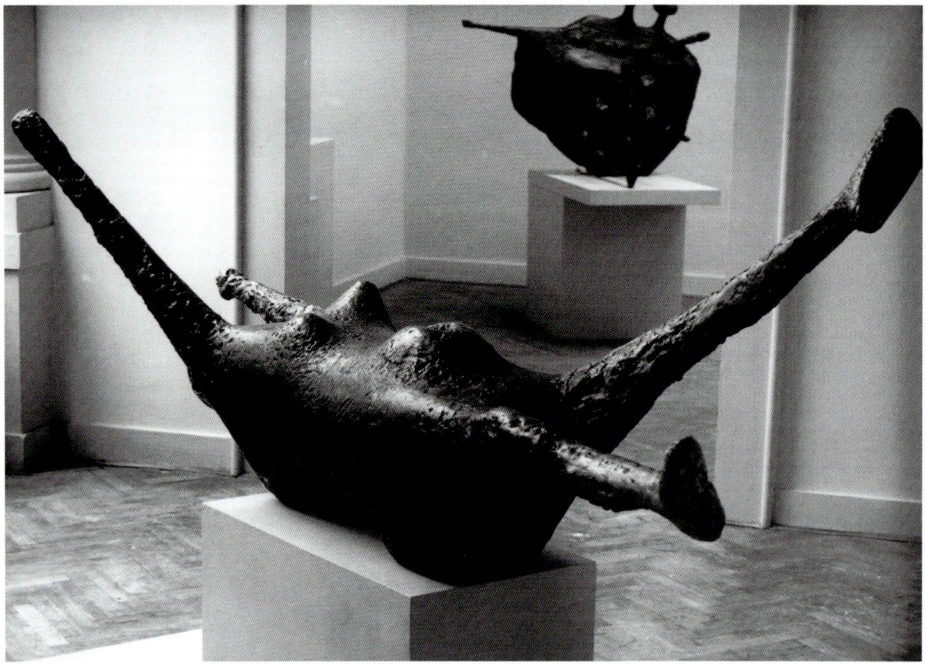

1958, British Pavilion, Venice Biennale, Kenneth Armitage

Photo by GIACOMELLI (Venezia)

Two Seated Figures, 1957
Bronze
Initialled `KA', dated and numbered from the edition of 6
32 x 43 x 31 cms (12½ x 17 x 12¼ in)

Provenance
Private collection, Denmark.

Literature
Kenneth Armitage - Life and Work, edited by Tamsyn Woollcombe, published by The Henry Moore Foundation in association with Lund Humphries, 1997, no. KA69.
The Sculpture of Kenneth Armitage, edited by James Scott, published by Lund Humphries, 2016, no. 71, p.111

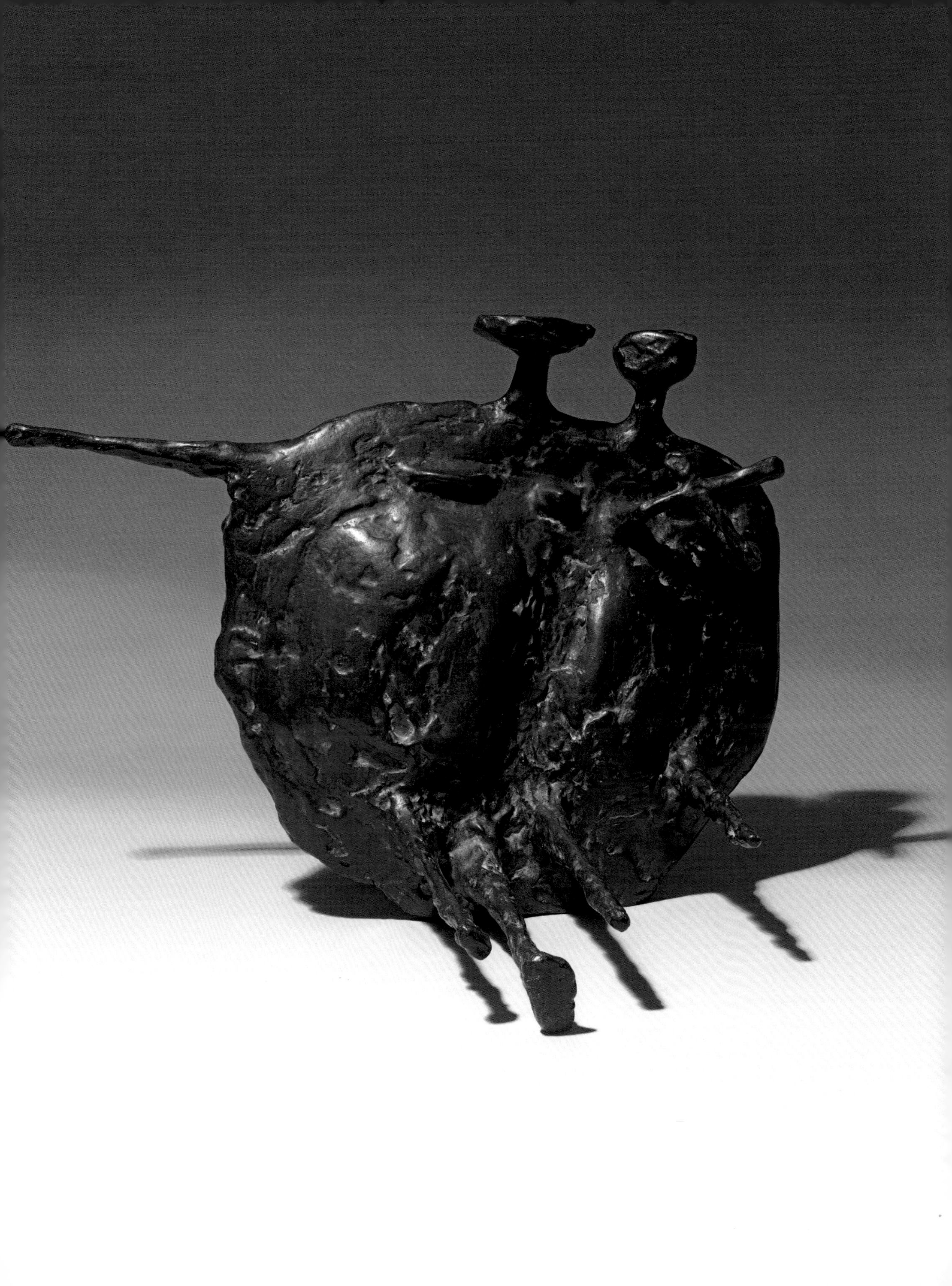

Robert Adams (1917-1984)

It was Reg Butler, not Robert Adams, who suggested that 'there is no such thing as abstract art .... The question of abstraction was one of degree. [Sculptors wished] to resolve their problems in a visual form, and this could not be called abstract art' at a discussion at the I.C.A's showing of 'London – Paris: new trends in painting and sculpture' in 1950. It characterised the tone of a continuing debate in early post-war years around the validity and relevance of definitions, and artists' desire to escape from dogmatic pigeon-holing in order to pursue their own explorations and creations, beyond critical judgments about belonging or not belonging to current movements and styles.

After an interrupted art college training, Adams had done his war service as an engineer, teaching himself to carve wood at the end of the war. His first sculptures in wood, plaster and eventually also stone bore some resemblance to the anthropomorphic vertical forms of Moore, veering between hollowed out rounded, meshed forms and assemblies of stacked irregularly shaped blocks, demonstrating a mastery of matters of weight and balance in his forms, in spite of the deliberate asymmetry of his figures. In the spirit of Moore's 'truth to material' credo, Adams showed particular sensitivity to the grain and structure of wood, just as he would in the way he exploited the natural properties of the metal forms he used in later works.

An interest in architecture and collaborating with architects would influence his direction towards 'construction'; and in that sense, by 1952 he stood out in Read's selection of sculptors for that Venice Biennale as the closest to 'geometry' but the furthest from 'fear'. For the ensuing five years, beginning with the series of exhibitions at the painter Adrian Heath's flat at 22 Fitzroy Street in London in 1952, Adams would exhibit with the Constructivists in a group around Victor Pasmore, Mary and Kenneth Martin, and Anthony Hill, but his work remained closer to the lyrical abstraction of Heath's painting rather than the strict geometric discipline being developed by the others. Adams' 'Vertical Construction' of 1951 still had superficial similarities with Butler's contemporary work – its verticality of course, but also transparency and the appearance of drawing in space – but already the irregular stacking of shaped planes anticipated Adams' spare, measured use of flat or curved linear forms.

Vertical Construction, 1951
Elm
Unique
119.4 x 20 x 20 cms (47 x 7¾ x 7¾ in)

Provenance
Collection of Kenneth Powell
Osborne Samuel, 2013
Private Collection, UK

Literature
The Sculpture of Robert Adams, Alastair Grieve, published by the Henry Moore Foundation in association with Lund Humphries, 1992, no. 119, p. 42 & 162

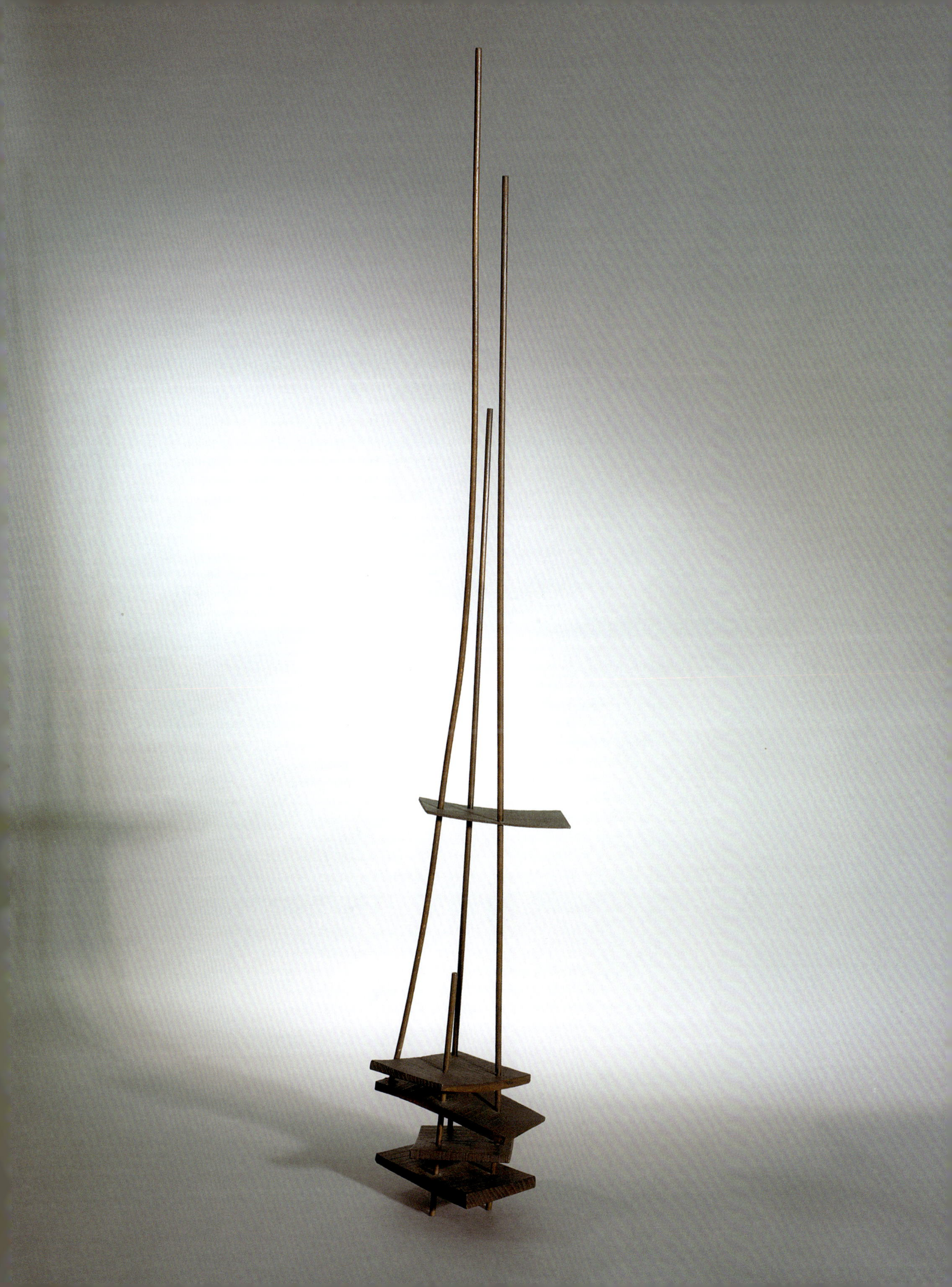

Robert Adams (1917-1984)

While continuing to work in wood and stone in the early 1950's he also learnt to weld, and began to exploit iron in its basic form of rods and sheets in order to assemble architecturally frontal sculptures. These would work as screens or reliefs rather than free-standing sculptures in the round. With one of his largest works to date, a free-standing relief called 'Monolithic Form' which foreshadows several works in the 1960's such as 'Vertical Screen Form' and indeed 'Opus 145', Adams explained: 'Monolithic Form is an attempt to create outdoor sculpture using simple abstract forms in relationship, the forms themselves creating the 'life' by their opposition to each other, as well as giving directions to certain thrusts and movements within the main form. These heavy angular forms were intended to contrast with and oppose the landscape rather than become one with it'.

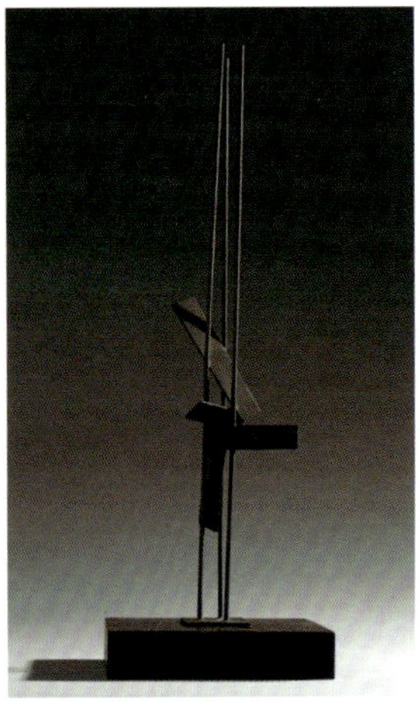

Maquette, 1962
Bronzed Steel
Unique
43.2 x 7.8 x 5.5 cms (17 x 3 x 2¼ in)

Exhibited
Gimpel fils, 1962, no.30

Provenance
Private Collection, USA
Private Collection, UK

Literature
The Sculpture of Robert Adams, Alastair Grieve, published by the Henry Moore Foundation in association with Lund Humphries, 1992, no. 422 (Opus 184), p.207

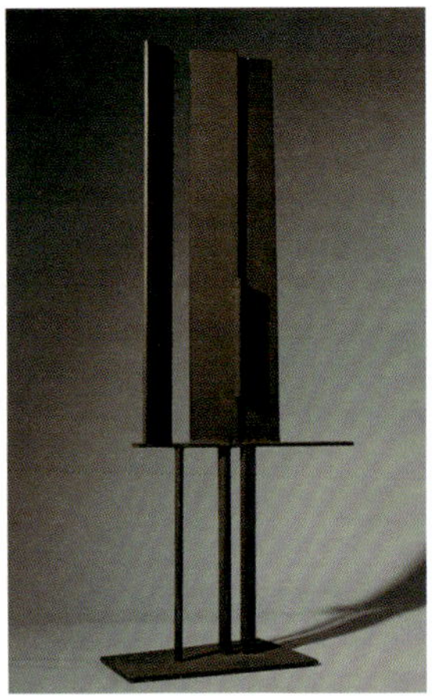

Left and right
Screen Form (Vertical), 1960
Bronze and steel
Unique
96 x 37.5 x 18.5 cms (37¾ x 14¾ x 7¼ in)

Exhibited
Gimpel fils, 1960, no 4

Literature
The Sculpture of Robert Adams, Alastair Grieve, published by the Henry Moore Foundation in association with Lund Humphries, 1992, no. 302 (Opus 93), p.191

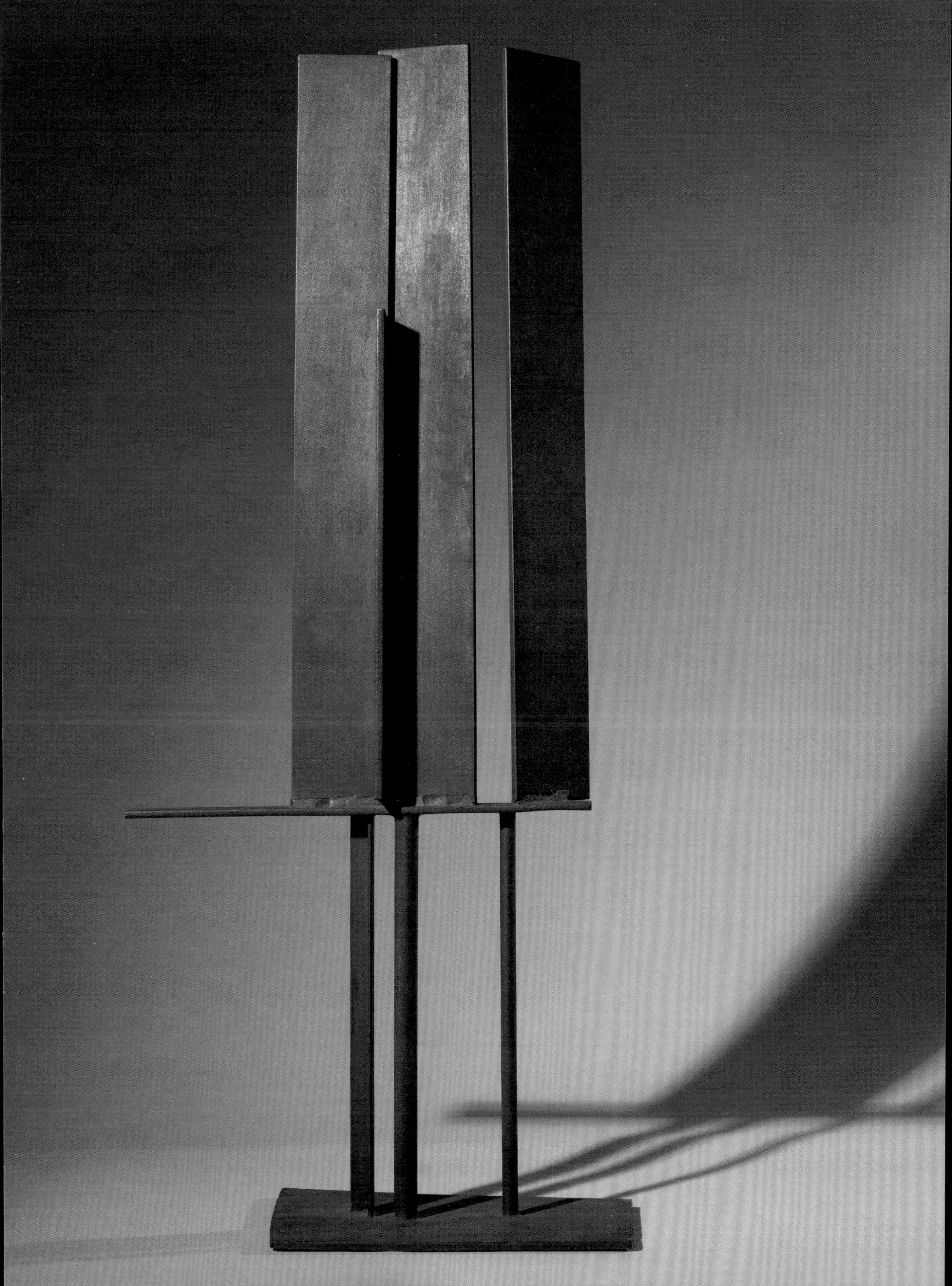

Robert Adams (1917-1984)

Of the 1952 Venice sculptors, only Paolozzi and Adams would participate in the now famous exhibition 'This is Tomorrow' at the I.C.A. in 1956. Adams collaborated with Frank Newby, Peter Carter and the architect Colin St John Wilson on a convex entrance 'tunnel' incorporating geometric elements in relief to form a sculptured three-dimensional, architectural environment. In 1957 Adams explained that as a consequence of this collaboration 'during the past year, forms in my work have changed from rectangular to curvilinear; solid mass and weight has given way to light linear forms and curved planes, and a fresh element – counterbalance – has appeared'.

This counterbalancing is seen in its fullest realization in the commission for a giant concrete relief screen to run the length of the new theatre in Gelsenkirchen in Germany, completed in 1969. In it Adams' angled projecting and receding elements create a measured rhythm of light and shadow, and of movement and stasis on a truly monumental scale.

Plane, Curve and Circle, 1960
Steel
Unique
230.5 x 54.6 x 38.5 cms (90½ x 21½ x 15¼ in)

Provenance
The Artist
Gimpel fils, London
Clossons, Cincinnati (acquired from the above in 1965)

Exhibited
Gimpel fils, London, 1960
The British Pavilion, XXXI Biennale, Venice, 1962

Literature
The Sculpture of Robert Adams, Alastair Grieve, published by the Henry Moore Foundation in association with Lund Humphries, 1992, no. 310 (Opus 102) p.86, 193 & 245

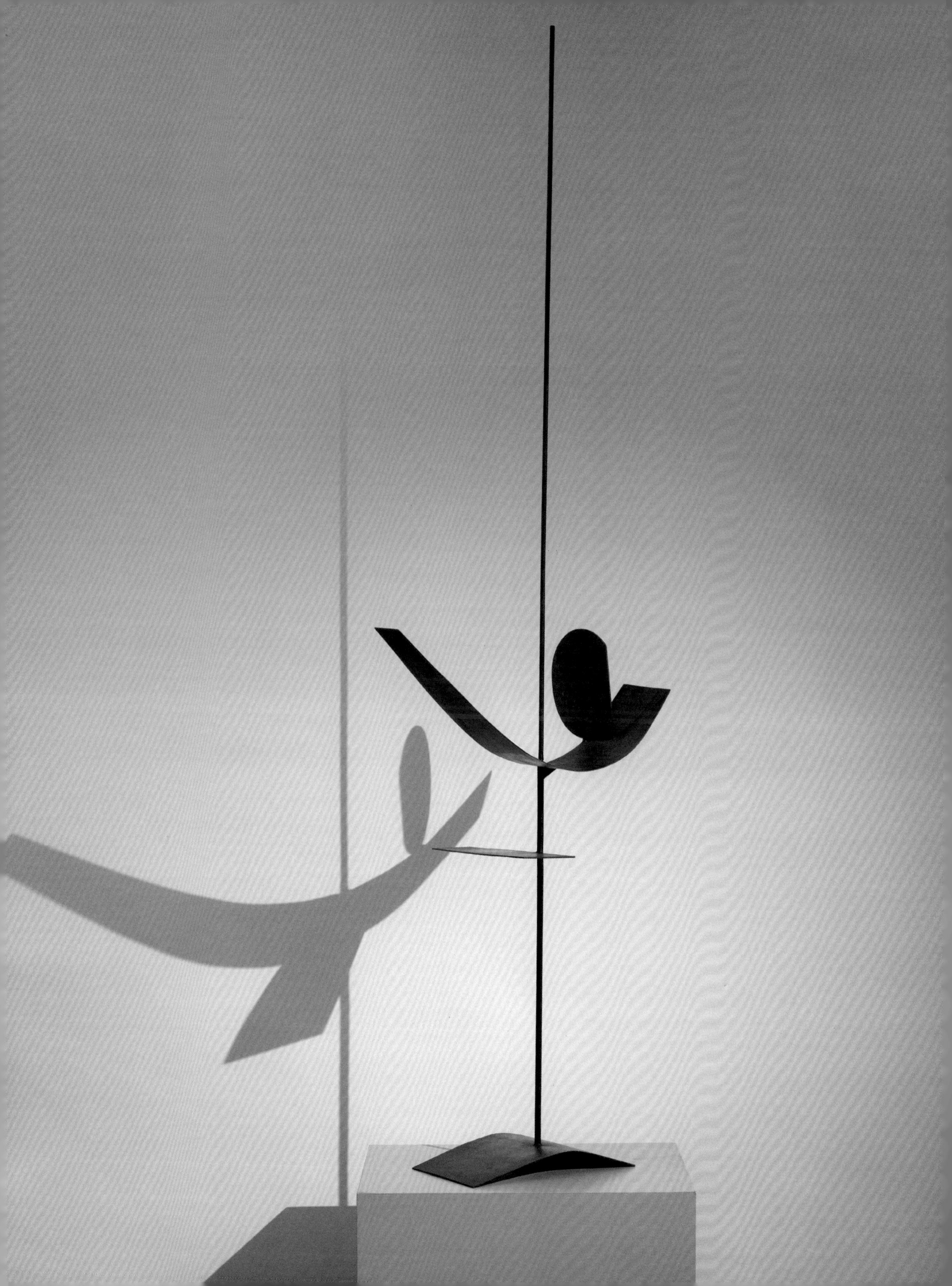

Robert Adams (1917-1984)

Curved Form (Rods), 1960
Bronze and steel
Unique
44.5 x 45.0 x 25.2 cms (17½ x 17¾ x 10 in)

Provenance
Gimpel fils (GF 16361)
Private Collection, UK

Exhibited
The British Pavilion, XXXI Biennale, Venice, 1962

Literature
The Sculpture of Robert Adams, Alastair Grieve, published by the Henry Moore Foundation in association with Lund Humphries, 1992, no. 337, p.196

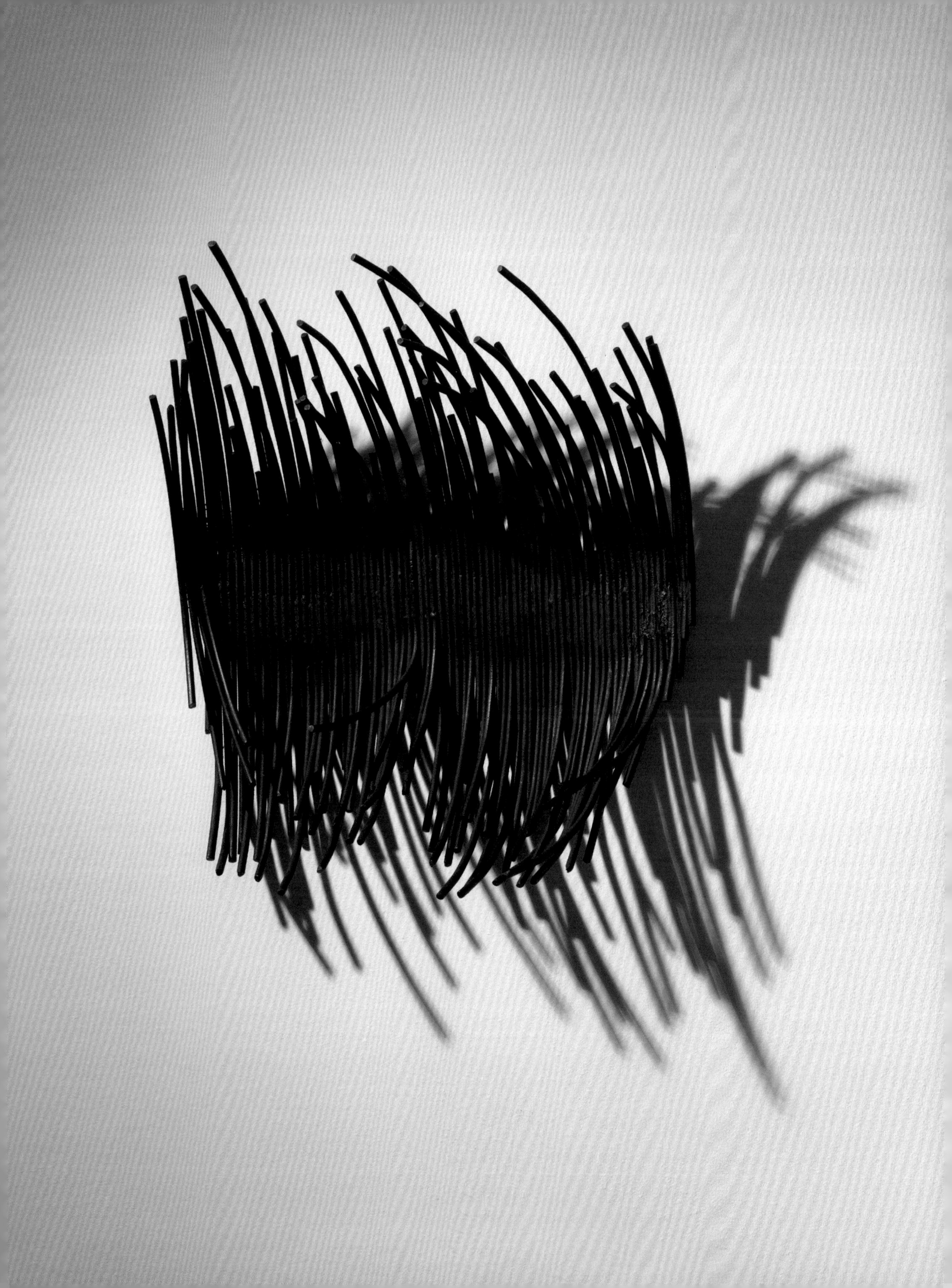

Robert Adams (1917-1984)

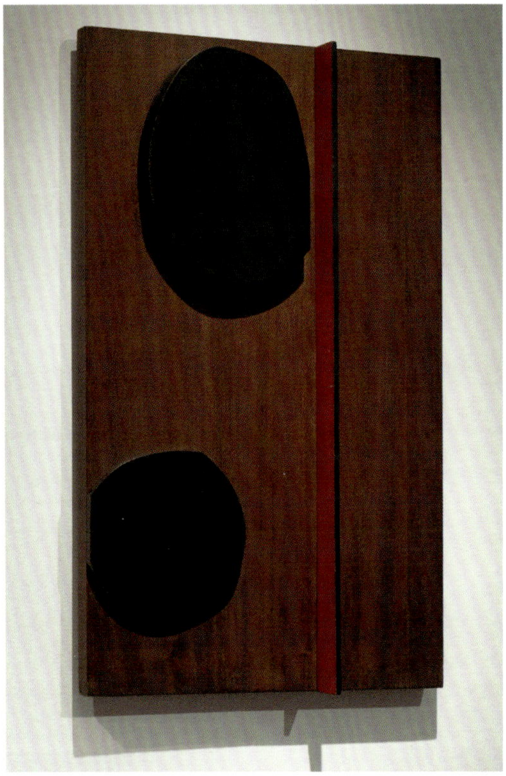

Two Circular Forms, Opus 214, 1964
Wood
Inscribed verso in pencil Robert Adams,
Two Circular Foms, 1964
61 x 38.1 x 5.5 cms (24 x 15 x 2¼ in)

Provenance
Gimpel fils (Reference GF7058)
Private collection, UK

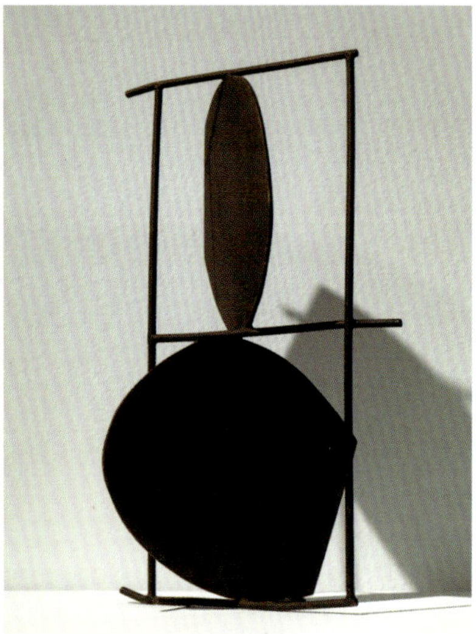

Maquette (Opus145), 1962
Stainless steel with pigment
Unique
24.1 x 13.5 x 10.1 cms (9½ x 5¼ x 4 in)

Provenance
Gimpel fils, London
Private Collection, UK, purchased from the above, 2006.

Literature
The Sculpture of Robert Adams, Alastair Grieve, published by the Henry Moore Foundation in association with Lund Humphries, 1992, no. 379, p.202

This is the maquette for Two Circular Forms No. 2, exhibited at the XXXI Biennale in Venice, 1962 when Adams represented Great Britain, now in the collection of the Galleria Nazionale d'Arte Moderna e Contemporanea, Rome.

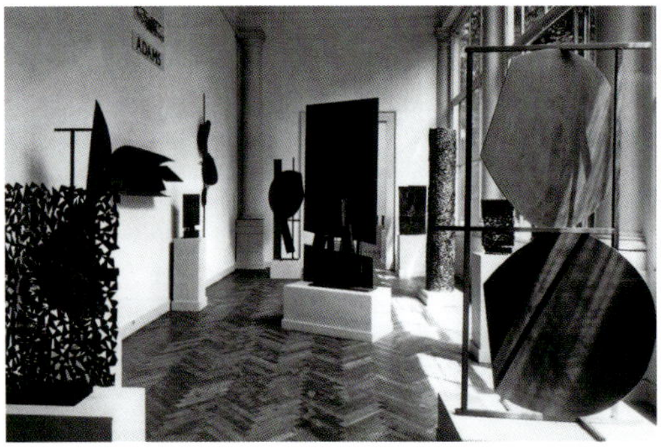

1962, British Pavilion, Venice Biennale, Robert Adams © Fondazione La Biennale di Venezia – Archivio Storico delle Arti Contemporanee. Photo by GIACOMELLI (Venezia)

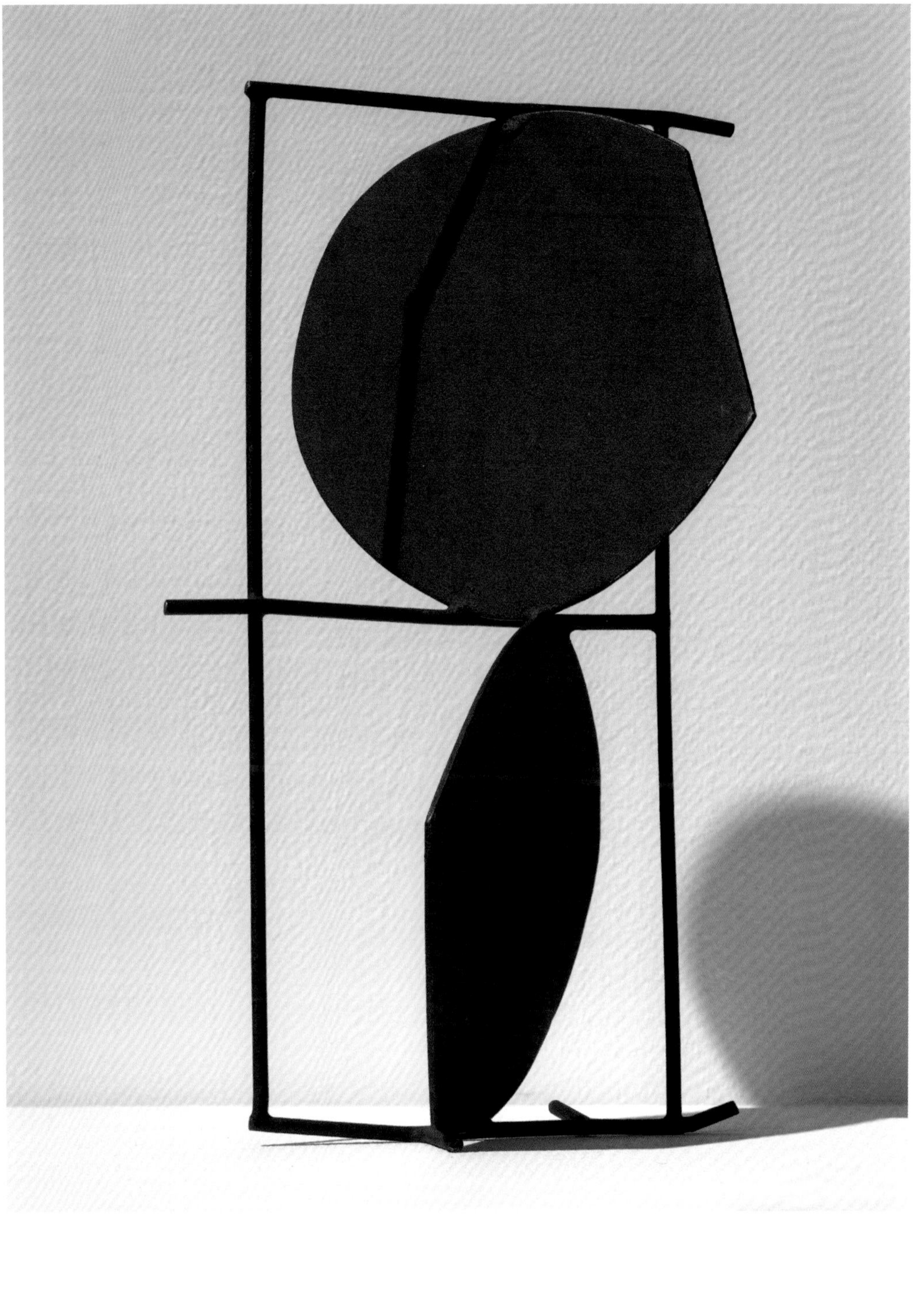

William Turnbull (1922-2012)

One might speak of three classic phases in Turnbull's oeuvre; of an early, middle and late period, with a transitional phase between the first and second, and a caesura between the second and third. His changes in style were not as coherent, nor of course as prolix, as those in Picasso's oeuvre, but they were similarly marked by the surprising contrast seen, say, between Picasso's cubist and classical works around 1916-18, or between his surrealist and sensuous ('Marie-Thérèse') works around 1929-32. An added dimension to Turnbull's work was his activity as a painter as well as a sculptor. His paintings had a particular role in signalling the transition he would make between the early and middle period, as they gradually eliminated the polychromy and the personal in his facture, anticipating the similar self-abnegation he would make in his sculpture.

After war service, while still studying at the Slade, together with his close friend and colleague Eduardo Paolozzi they decided to 'escape' to Paris for two years in 1947-49, absorbing the influences particularly of Giacometti on the one hand, and Brancusi on the other. Throughout his artistic career, Turnbull was to maintain an interest in, and assemble his own modest collection of, primitive art: masks, figurines and ritual objects of undefinable use.

Eve 1, 1959
Bronze and East Indian (Sonokeling) Rosewood
Stamped with the artist's monogram and dated '59' at base of bronze part
Unique
156.2 x 38.1 cms (61½ x 15 in)

Provenance
E.J. Power
Thence by family descent
Waddington Galleries, London
Private Collection, UK

Exhibited
William Turnbull: Sculpture, Molton Gallery, London, 19 April-6 May 1960, catalogue no.9 (repro. in b&w) (incorrectly captioned 'Eve 2')
William Turnbull: sculpture and painting, The Tate Gallery, London, 15 August-7 October 1973, catalogue no.47, p.40 (repro. in b&w p.41)
William Turnbull: Beyond Time, Waddington Galleries, London, 9 June-3 July 2010, catalogue no.13 (repro. in colour p.[45])

Literature
Expositions: Grande-Bretagne, review of Molton Gallery exhibition, J.P. Hodin, Quadrum: Revue Internationale d'Art Moderne, no.11, December 1961, p.175 (repro. in b&w)
The Sculpture and Painting of William Turnbull, Lawrence Alloway, Art International, vol.5, no.1, 1 February 1961, pp.46-52 (repro. in b&w p.47, fig.4)
The Sculpture of William Turnbull, Amanda A. Davidson, The Henry Moore Foundation in association with Lund Humphries, 2005, catalogue no.93, pp.50 & 108 (repro. in b&w p.108)

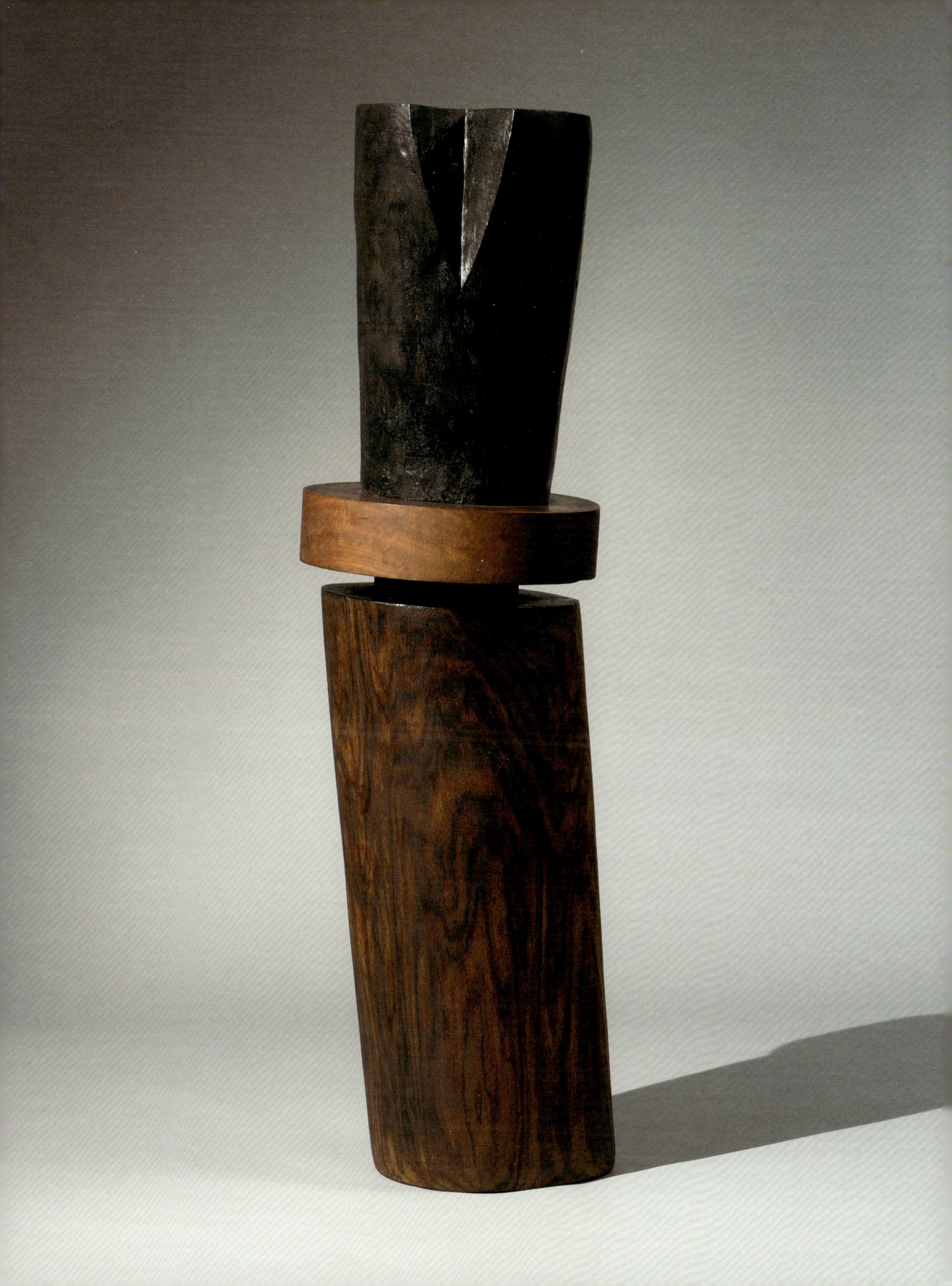

William Turnbull (1922-2012)

In the early phase until around 1962-63, his work would have less to do with Herbert Read's assessment of British sculptors' fears, or indeed with Dubuffet's consecration of graffiti at the Foyer de l'Art Brut in Paris, but rather with the existential isolation of the figure and the elemental, instinctual carving and marking of totem-like forms which resonated with his interest in primitive art. Turnbull produced idol figures in plaster (for eventual casting in bronze), whose appearance of hand-built forming and whose hand-drawn striations would contrast with his clearly Brancusi-inspired totems assembled from basic columnar or ovoid shapes in wood, metal and stone.

Whether it was his predisposition to analyse and simplify forms in sculpture, his increasing reduction and purification of mark-making in his painting, or the encounter with the work of American sculptors such as David Smith or Donald Judd, his middle period of sculpture in the 1960s brought him to an extreme moment of impersonality where he was laying out industrial elements on the floor in rigid geometry in the non plus ultra of a minimalist ethic. A crisis ensued, whereby he stopped making work in the early 1970's for three years, before beginning again with small hand-formed and marked bronzes, referencing once again the primitive arts that he had continued to collect. He would eventually combine the hand-formed with deliberately chosen, unsophisticated found elements in structures that recalled the human form, but which appeared to be reconstituted as if from whatever could be found left lying around discarded. Whether this was a final statement, or a stage in the continuing search for a synthesis of the primitive with the detritus of modern civilization, was left in the end for others to decide.

Female Figure, 1988
Bronze
Signed and numbered from the edition of 6
The maquette *Study for Female Figure* was conceived in 1960 (Ref: no.98)
190.5 x 101.6 x 50.8 cms (74¾ x 40 x 20 in)

Provenance
Waddington Galleries Ltd, London
Private Collection USA, purchased from the above in 1989
Private Collection, Switzerland

Exhibited
Waddington Galleries, Solo exhibition, 1991, cat 9 (illus. p.23)

Literature
Davidson, Amanda, *The Sculpture of William Turnbull*, published by Lund Humphries, 2005, p.175, no. 263

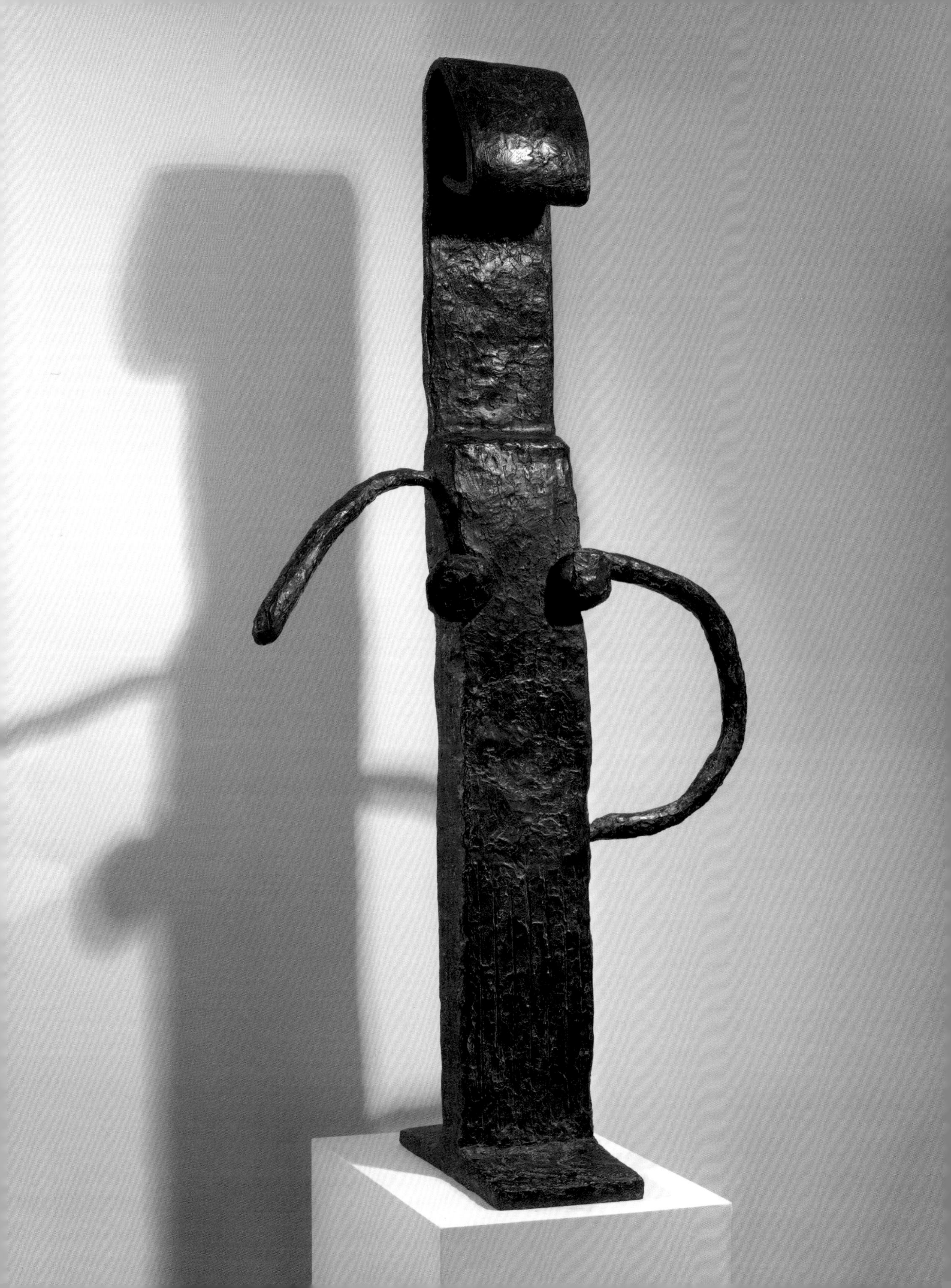

Geoffrey Clarke (1924-2014)

Among the Venice Biennale sculptors Geoffrey Clarke was almost certainly the one who carried to completion the greatest number of public commissions in the first two decades after the war, often in successful collaboration with architects. Before 1960, his work appeared to have elements of the brittle, spiky, tortured extrusions that recurred in the work of some of his fellow sculptors of that generation. He, Turnbull and Paolozzi were about ten years younger than Butler and his contemporaries, and they themselves were about ten years younger than Moore and Hepworth. Clarke's sculptures, however, had their origins in different sources from the other exhibitors at that Biennale, carried different meanings for him personally, and were also intended to suggest different connections to the viewer.

Unlike Chadwick, who admitted to an unusual reversal of the stages of making work – Chadwick said that he often began with a full-scale sculpture, then might decide to make smaller versions as maquettes, and only then might execute some related drawings or prints – Clarke's ideas for his sculpture originated in his graphic work. He explained that his graphic language was inspired by some casual doodles he had seen by Picasso, which Clarke then developed in his own drawings and deeply etched black and white aquatints. Most depicted vertical, plant-like forms with spindly unsteady outgrowths which for him represented a human figure with stylized head and limbs. Clarke produced a number of such chamber-music-scale, drawings-derived iron sculptures during the 1950's, 'Fawn' with its low-rising tendrils suggesting the elfin-like character of the sprightly mythological creature.

The etchings owed much to the graphic work of Paul Klee, and not a little to Graham Sutherland, too. The sources of Clarke's motifs were drawn, in quasi-neo-Romantic vein from seeds, seedpods and their germination, which he had explored in the displays at the Natural History Museum, just as his 'Spirit of Electricity' sculpture would also draw on his exploration of the displays on lighting and early radar at the Science Museum.

After beginning art studies at colleges in the North of England which were interrupted by the war, Clarke continued his studies afterwards at the Royal College of Art in London; at first in the stained glass department, then he moved over to the sculpture department.

The Spirit of Electricity Maquette, 1958-59
Iron and brass
Unique
78.5 x 7.5 x 7.7 cms (30¾ x 3 x 3 in)

Provenance
Sir Jules Thorn
Mrs P Rodd (designer at Thorn House)
Private Collection, UK

Commissioned for Thorn House by the architect Sir Basil Spence (Sir Basil was appointed the co-ordinating architect of the Festival of Britain). The final version of *The Spirit of Electricity* is 240 cm in height and is still visible on the now renamed building Orion House, Upper St Martin's Lane, London.

To be included in the forthcoming *Geoffrey Clarke Sculptor: A Catalogue Raisonne* by Judith LeGrove, published by Lund Humphries, Nov 2017.

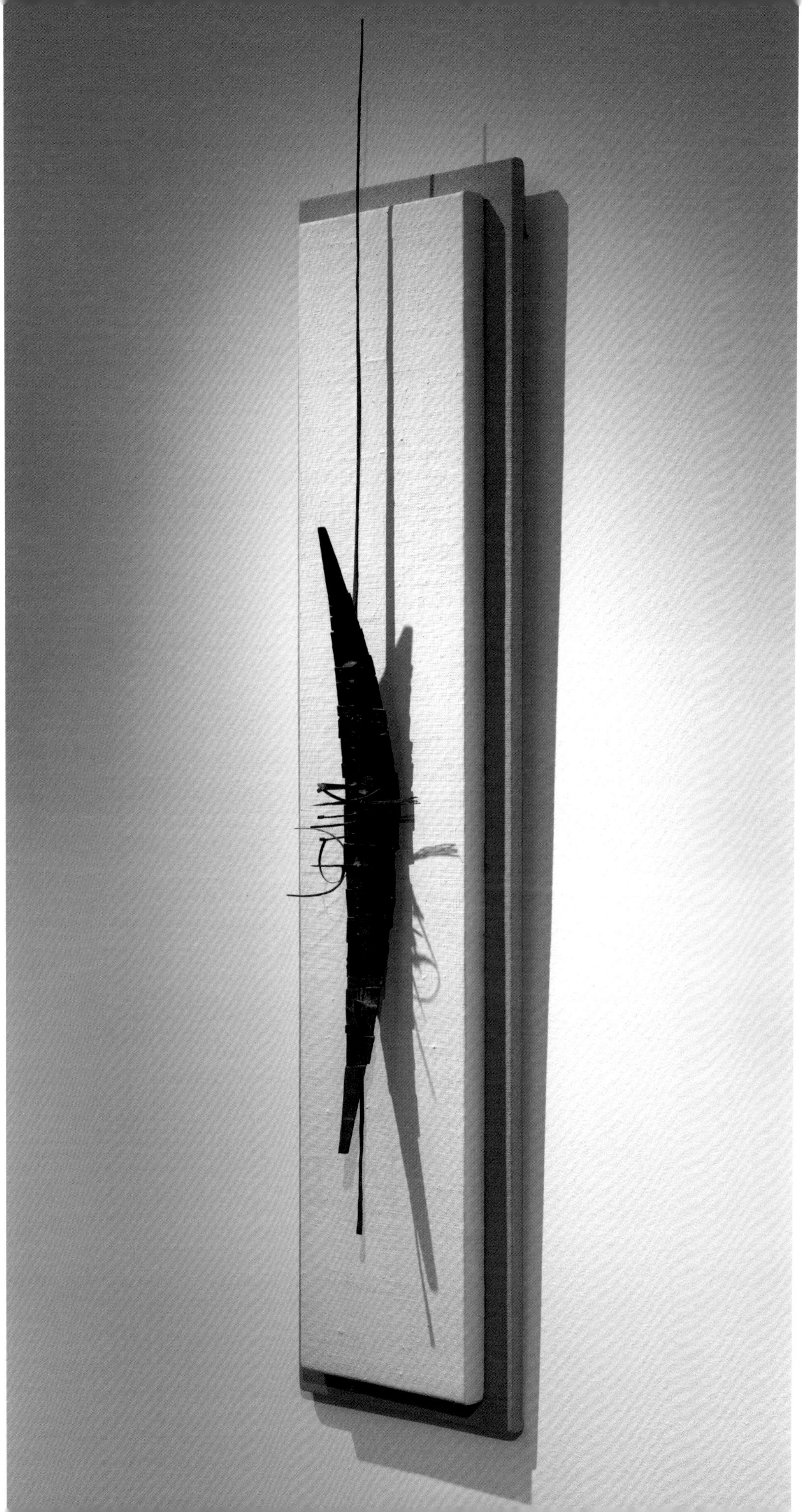

Geoffrey Clarke (1924-2014)

However he found its concentration on clay and plaster modelling unsatisfying, and transferred to the wood, metal and plastics department. Like Butler and Chadwick, he found that using iron, forged and welded, worked best for the speed of execution he sought, and allowed direct control of the process of making, in preference to bronze casting. Considering his modest means, too, iron was cheap, came in the form of rods which were convenient to work with – especially in adapting to the upright forms which he wanted to build – and had none of the precious appearance and lengthy, complicated procedures that came with bronze casting. In 1953, the critic Lawrence Alloway would highlight these three sculptors' work in a survey entitled 'Britain's new Iron Age'.

In 1951 Clarke travelled to France, visiting churches in Caen, Chartres and Matisse's chapel in Vence, to look at stained glass in preparation for work on Coventry's new Cathedral. He would achieve fame with the works commissioned by Basil Spence for this building which, in a manner similar to the recently staged Festival of Britain, would become a symbol of the country's recovery and forward-looking identity after the war. Work began in 1952 on the site adjoining that of the 14th century cathedral destroyed in the devastating bombing in November 1940, and would not be finally completed until ten years later, by which time Clarke had contributed three stained glass windows in the nave, the High Altar's cross, a Crown of Thorns and a Flying Cross for the cathedral itself, as well as another cross and candlesticks for its undercroft.

While involved with the work on the cathedral, Clarke was also commissioned by Thorn Electrical Industries to produce a wall sculpture for their new headquarters building in St Martin's Lane in London. The maquette for the design, exhibited here, still referred to the idea of growth with its projecting rods which tailed off in uneven lengths, set against an African shield-like reflector to suggest the reception and emission of different wavelengths that silently saturate the air beyond our sight and hearing. This proved to be a mammoth undertaking, requiring the full-size eighty-foot wood and fibreglass model to be assembled in his studio in Suffolk, before being handed over to a bronze foundry to be cast in sections, over which he felt he had little control. He would only make one more such over-large bronze wall sculpture – a giant flower planted in a table – for Bishop Otter College in Chichester in the following year, before decisively abandoning iron and bronze in favour of more malleable aluminium for his new landscape-inspired, folded sculptural forms.

Fawn, 1951
Iron
Unique
10 x 13.5 x 5.2 cms (4 x 5¼ x 2 in)

Provenance
Private Collection, UK

Exhibited
Gimpel fils, `Geoffrey Clarke', 1952, no.39

To be included in the forthcoming *Geoffrey Clarke Sculptor: A Catalogue Raisonne* by Judith LeGrove, published by Lund Humphries, Nov 2017.

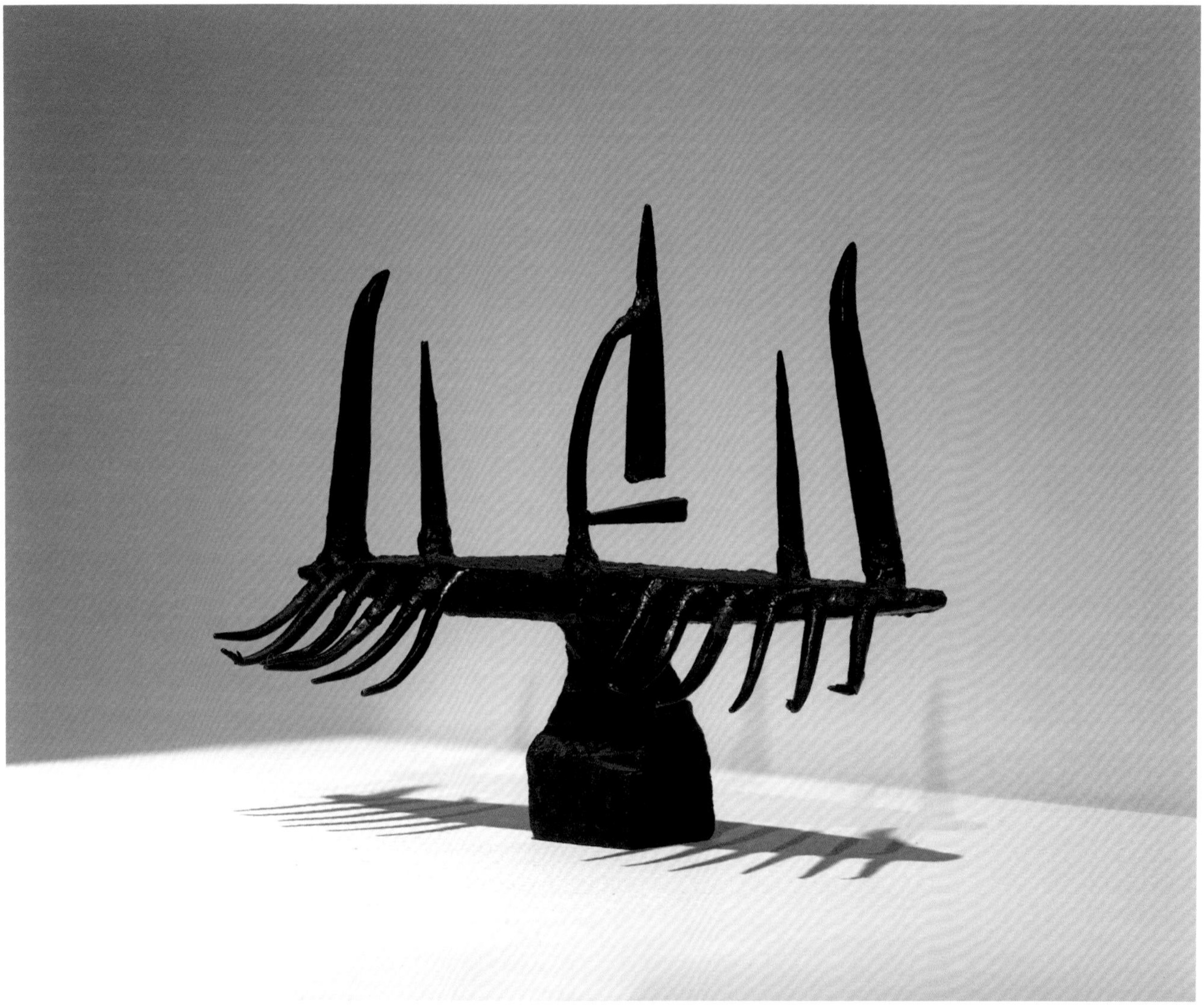

Eduardo Paolozzi (1924-2005)

Among the eight sculptors Read chose for the 1952 Venice Biennale,Paolozzi appeared to be the one least tied to the traditional language of sculpture and its materials.

As an Italo-Scot who had lost members of his family drowned as they were being transported by sea to internment in Canada during the war, at that early stage in his life he felt an outsider to British society. Although he attended art colleges in Edinburgh, Oxford and London between 1943 and 1947 (interrupted by a brief episode of war service) he soon declared his position in relation to then current modern British sculpture, pronouncing on Moore: '...a continual source of surprise and inspiration ... However, he is still a man of the 30's, and the idea of holes in wood for sculpture is not for us today'.

From the start of his career as an artist, Paolozzi was investigating an eclectic range of sources of inspiration. In 1944, he had been inspired by Schwitters' exhibition of paintings, collages and sculptures at Jack Bilbo's Modern Art Gallery in London. Read had written in the exhibition catalogue 'Schwitters has shown that it is possible to make art out of anything – so long as one is an artist. Used train tickets, pieces of cardboard, or corrugated paper, corks, matches, rags – all is grist to the creative imagination, and Schwitters has pursued this line of development far beyond the point reached by Picasso. Schwitters is the supreme master of collage'. This original Dada-ist's iconoclastic spirit of art-making would permeate the spirit of Paolozzi's own work for a long time. At the Slade (at that time relocated to Oxford), he befriended William Turnbull, Richard Hamilton and Nigel Henderson, who would form the core of the 'Independent Group' [the I.G.].

They would explore science, natural history and ethnographic collections, Paolozzi believing that 'the neglect of 'the primitive' was part of a wider English insularity'. And preferring enterprising private galleries' exhibitions to the more conventional public ones, Henderson recalled: '[Paolozzi] seemed to understand with formidable clarity that art was not to be derived constantly from art in polite circles for polite people, but rescued and fused from the enormous mass of material ... from the specific cornucopia of our time'. The premise of the I.C.A's second-ever exhibition in 1948, '40,000 years of Modern Art', chimed with his and some other contemporary artists' understanding of the raw, unmediated creativity they believed to be embodied in art of primitive or very ancient cultures.

Paolozzi's first exhibition at the Mayor Gallery in the previous year, when he had shown drawings and concrete reliefs, was such a success that he was able to stay for two years in Paris on the proceeds, joining up with Turnbull, and meeting artists such as Brancusi, Giacometti, Arp, Léger, and particularly Dubuffet.

Figure, 1955-56
Bronze
31.8 x 20.0 x 12.0 cms (12½ x 7¾ x 4¾ in)

Provenance
Private Collection, USA
Private Collection, UK

Literature
Collins, Judith, *Eduardo Paolozzi*, published by Lund Humphries, 2014, p.125 cat no. 107. (titled Standing Figure)

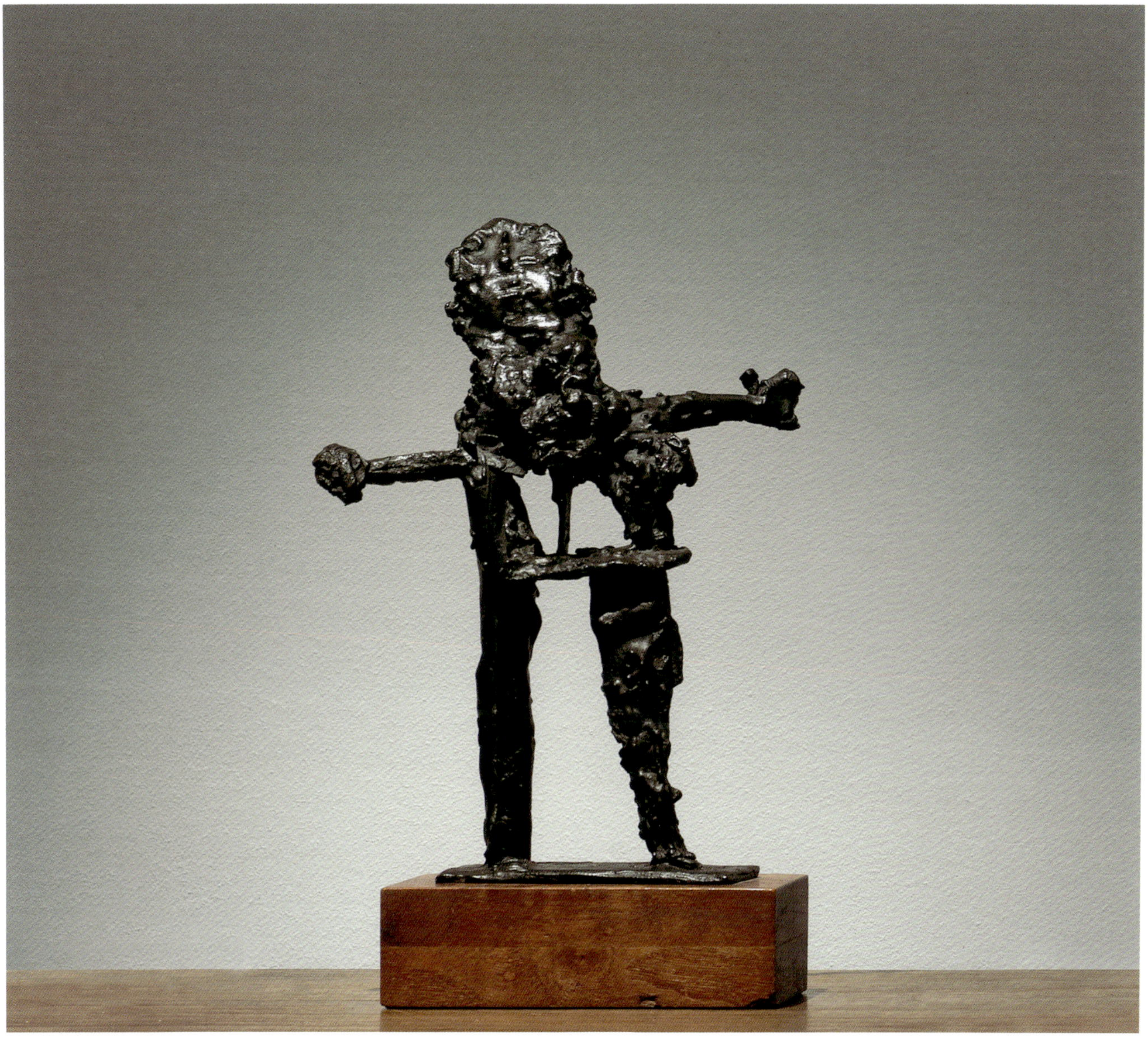

Eduardo Paolozzi (1924-2005)

Seeing the latter's exhibition at the Galerie René Drouin, and encountering his Foyer de l'Art Brut, installed in that gallery's basement, reinforced his view that 'everything that came to hand could be material for his art'. Before returning from Paris to Britain, did he perhaps see Drouin's programme-defining exhibition 'L'Art brut préferé aux arts culturels', which encompassed 200 works by 63 outsider artists, or Pierre Loeb's presentation of drawings by the famous dramatist and proponent of a 'Theatre of Cruelty', Antonin Artaud. For that exhibition, Loeb had written, 'I'm waiting for an art that's ungrateful, ugly, crude, as painful as giving birth, because it's a question of birth, not of games any longer, here as elsewhere'.

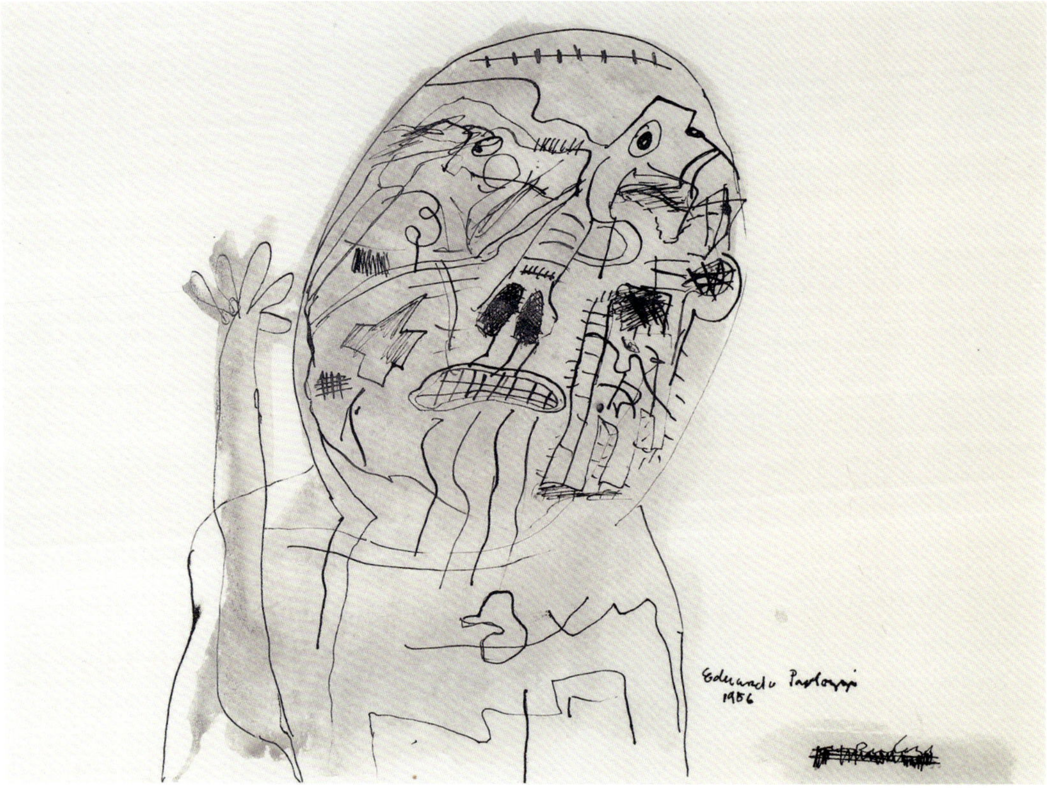

Figure with Raised Arm, 1956
Ink & wash
Signed and dated lower right
27.9 x 38.1 cms (11 x 15 in)

Provenance
Private Collection, USA
Private Collection, UK

Literature
Collins, Judith, *Eduardo Paolozzi*, published by Lund Humphries, 2014. p.109 cat no. 87

As Hamilton later explained, justifying the I.G.'s policy of avoiding making value judgements; 'we were able to say everything we think of is right and can be used', and claiming for the group: 'if there was one binding spirit amongst the people at the I.G. it was a distaste for Herbert Read's attitudes', referring to that critic's notion of art as a transcendent and a-historical manifestation. Paolozzi was undeterred in the breadth of his scavenging, fascinated as many in the I.G. also were by Hollywood cinema and the imagery of American sci-fi and comic magazines. These he was able to obtain from G.I.s in Paris, and would turn their popular and at times lurid imagery into his prescient, proto-Pop collages which he first showed at the I.C.A. in 1952.

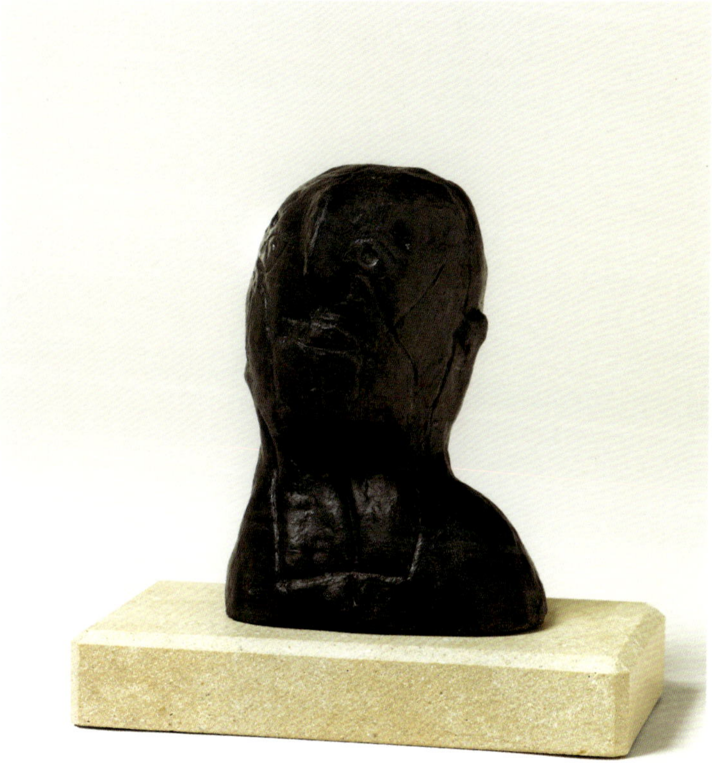

Head, 1951
Bronze
Dated and signed on the back of the head
13.5 x 9.8 x 7.0 cms (5¼ x 3¾ x 2¾ in)

Provenance
The Artist
Sir Colin St John Wilson, acquired from the above
Private Collection, UK

Literature
Collins, Judith, *Eduardo Paolozzi*, published by Lund Humphries, 2014. p.104 cat no. 79. (Titled Small Head and dated 1953)

Eduardo Paolozzi (1924-2005)

Collage, as he later defined it, should 'damage, erase, destroy, deface and transform – all parts of a metaphor for the creative act itself'. He would later adapt his definition of collage for his approach to the sculptures he was developing in the mid-1950's.

He began to experiment with metal casting around 1949, when the impact of Surrealism and of the encounter with Giacometti was still vivid. However, taking up the teaching post in textiles at the Central School of Arts and Crafts in London seems to have initiated a tapestry of graffiti-like scrawlings in his figurative as much as in his abstract drawings, and to have suggested an appliqué technique of patches of clay, basted-together into the sculptures of heads, which he would cast in bronze in the early 1950's. Of these, the young art critic Robert Melville wrote: 'It is as if the artist had worked in the atmosphere of the street accident and the brutal holdup, subjecting the heads not to what is called a merciless insight into character, but to a violent physical assault'.

After the Heads series, Paolozzi proceeded to assemble clay fragments into small mutilated bodies with stretched limbs and crushed torsos – as if they could almost be three-dimensional renderings of the figures in Dubuffet's contemporary paintings – and he cast them in bronze, too. By 1956 the experience of assembling sculptures from found fragments would lead to the formidable series of almost life-size figures named after mythical Greek heroes, whose surface textures were tapestried with impressions of discarded wheels, toys, clocks, dolls, and other debris, as if these had simply been gathered up and hastily glued together in a fit of enthusiasm. Paolozzi explained: 'I am interested, above all, in investigating the golden ability of the artist to achieve a metamorphosis of quite ordinary things into something wonderful and extraordinary that is neither nonsensical nor morally edifying'. Ever searching and questioning, around 1960 this new, morally neutral playfulness would lead Paolozzi to surprise his followers by composing quasi-symmetrical solid sculptural objects from machined and sometimes also painted metal components that had no significant purpose or meaning other than their own corporeal presence.

Daedalus, 1990
Bronze with brown patina
Signed, dated twice & inscribed 'Unikat' verso
Cast at Arch Bronze Foundry, London in 1990
Five slightly varying versions recorded, this unique work was the first one.
(other versions are within the collections at the Tate, London,
Scottish National Gallery of Modern Art, Edinburgh and Jesus College, Cambridge.)
157 x 54 x 40 cms (61¾ x 21¼ x 15¾ in)

This work is recorded in the archives compiled by Professor Robin Spencer.

Provenance
Private Collection, Switzerland

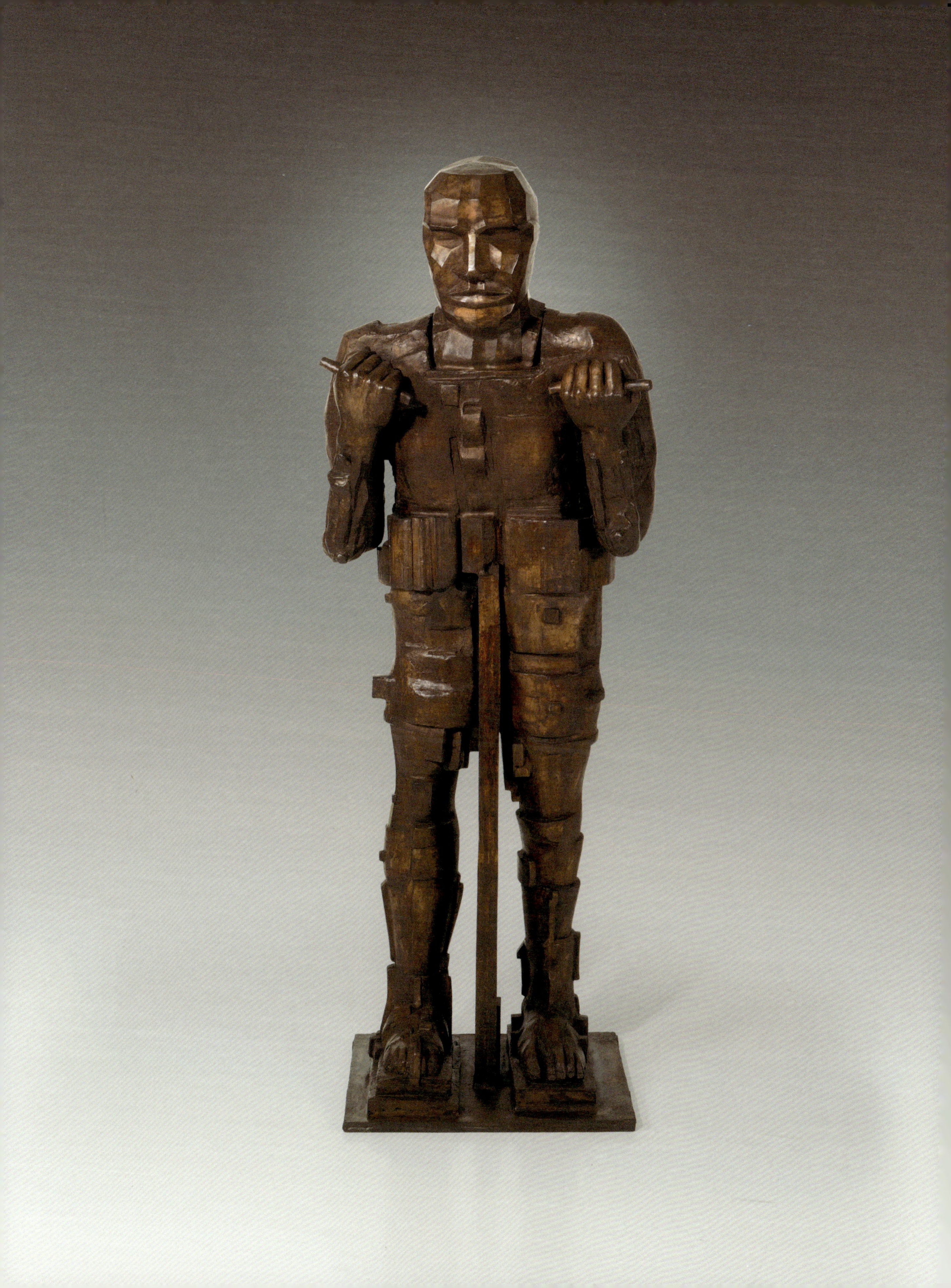

A brief overview of some influential figures in the British art world after 1945

In the second chapter of her magisterial study of art in Britain 'New Art, New World: British art in post-war society', Margaret Garlake examined the art support systems that evolved during the war, and would become established in the ensuing decade. Any brief summary here cannot substitute for her scholarship but could still outline the complexity of the interrelated institutions, individuals and emerging trends that influenced developments in the world of contemporary art in Britain in those early post-war years, and encourage the reader to look back into Garlake's book.

Where to begin? Two seminal figures stand out, especially since with their activity and advocacy they also link the 1930's with the 1950's. The first, Herbert Read (1893 - 1968), academic, poet, writer, art historian and critic, collector, ceramicist and anarchist, had been engaging with contemporary British and continental art since the 1920's, befriending and supporting Moore and Hepworth's generation, through Nash and Piper, 1930's Surrealists and Constructivists (in preference to Sutherland and the neo-Romantics) up to 'his' post-war 'Geometry of fear' generation. He would become humorously known as 'the Pope of Modern Art'. The second would be Kenneth Clark (1903 - 1983), also known somewhat humorously as 'Lord Clark of Civilisation' for the television series which he presented in 1969, depicting a history principally of Western art as 'Civilisation' but which would be criticised before long for being mainly only about white, male, Western art.

As the son of wealthy parents, Clark enjoyed privileged social connections, and with his precocious talent as an art historian and protégé of the 'Pope' of Italian Renaissance studies Bernard Berenson, he was appointed director of the National Gallery at the age of 30. Clark's own eclectic art collection included Old Masters through to 19th century French art, Bloomsbury, the Euston Road School and the neo-Romantics, but avoided Surrealism and Abstraction. Clark was instrumental in setting up the War Artists Advisory Committee and would take over from a third seminal figure, the former Bloomsbury member, economist, academic and art collector John Maynard Keynes, who chaired the wartime organization CEMA (the Committee for Encouragement of Music and the Arts) and oversaw its transformation into the Arts Council of Great Britain in 1946, but died in the same year. The newly appointed Director of the British Council's art department in 1947, Lillian Somerville, is a fourth seminal figure, for her courageous and tireless promotion of contemporary British art exhibitions around the world for the next 25 years or so.

Some privately wealthy collectors and influential patrons, such as the Surrealist and friend of Picasso, Roland Penrose, the visionary dilettante Peter Watson, and Eric Gregory, the director of the art publishing firm Lund Humphries, were the prime movers and occasionally rescue-funders of the Institute of Contemporary Arts, which they founded in 1947, together with Herbert Read, Geoffrey Grigson and E.L.T.Mesens. It not only presented experimental and interdisciplinary art exhibitions, but also programmes of music, lectures, seminars and so on, with limited support from the Arts Council whose more cautious programmes it initially challenged. When Bryan Robertson became director of the Whitechapel Art Gallery in 1952, his adventurous exhibition programme, presenting leading contemporary figures of European and American art also challenged the Arts Council to greater ambition. Many of these figures would eventually be co-opted into the public arts-promoting institutions in rotating roles, as were some leading artists such as Henry Moore, or Directors of art schools such as William Coldstream.

Who weren't co-opted, however, were the art dealers, since their support for living artists was felt to be tainted by commercial interests, and public institutions' limited exhibitions and prizes were thought, perhaps questionably, to be more beneficial for artists. The impact of some dealers should not be ignored, however, for their discovery and support of young British artists, by introducing them and promising foreign artists to the British public, and for their contacts and collaboration with dealers abroad. Both before and after the war, the Leicester Galleries, Reid & Lefèvre, and sporadically the Mayor, London and Zwemmer galleries presented contemporary French and even some German art, and then after the war Peter and Charles Gimpel, Erica Brausen at the Hanover Gallery and Rex Nan Kivell at the Redfern were leading promoters of the new generation of British sculptors and painters, without neglecting to show new talent from abroad as well. Gradually a number of not exactly fringe but still adventurous galleries with more parlous finances appeared, such as Helen Lessore's Beaux Arts Gallery, Denis Bowen's New Vision Gallery, or Victor Musgrave's Gallery One. This would be before the 1960's explosion of fun and adventure with dealers such as John Kasmin, Robert Fraser and the designer Terence Conran's 'Habitat' enterprise.

Lastly, one should remember the role of committed advocates and progressive provocateurs, who might be artists, writers or academics, such as Alan Bowness, the art historian and influential lecturer at the Courtauld Institute, who 'trained' many graduate and post-graduate students who would take up art museum or gallery posts in the expansion years of the 1960's and 1970's, and his colleague, David Sylvester, who chose to maintain his independence as a critic, writer and exhibition organizer, as did Lawrence Alloway, a vociferous supporter of abstraction and then emerging Pop Art, before he moved to America in 1961. These academics and critics, as well as some senior figures from universities or art schools, would also rotate as chairmen or members of these public arts institutions' boards or committees, tending to cement a certain consensus view of what was worthy of public patronage and what was not, until independent voices began to be heard questioning this unanimity in the 1970's.

Alloway was also a member of the 'Independent Group', incubated within the I.C.A., which included the artist Richard Hamilton, a formidable innovator in exhibition ideas and design. With Victor Pasmore and Harry Thubron, Hamilton devised the influential Bauhaus-inspired Basic Design course at King's College, Durham, where they taught. And perhaps one of the most overlooked innovators of the post-war period was the Scottish artist William Johnstone, Principal of Camberwell School of Art from 1938, before he moved on to direct the Central School of Arts and Crafts from 1947 to 1962. He developed the practice, already pioneered in collaboration with Victor Pasmore at Camberwell, of bringing in young artists of promise to teach in departments which were deliberately not their area of chosen work, such as Paolozzi who taught in the textile department, Alan Davie in jewellery, and Nigel Henderson in photography. This new practice would be taken up in differing ways by William Coldstream at the Slade, and Clifford Ellis at the Bath Academy of Art. Noticeable in all this is the low profile in the immediate post-war period of the impoverished Tate Gallery, which only won its very first, paltry purchase grant of £2000 from the Treasury in 1948, but which, through its sympathetic director John Rothenstein, would host many of the Arts Council's most important exhibitions in the period before the Hayward Gallery finally opened its doors in 1968.

Afterthought

The international prestige attained by British sculpture post-war may also be due in part to the extent to which so many of the European continent's living artists had been censored, silenced, exiled or compromised by the war. Furthermore, across the continent so much of the 'infrastructure' for making and distributing art had been damaged or interrupted by invasion, occupation and the destruction of physical premises. As a consequence the networks of artists' associations, galleries and publications had also been severely disrupted, persecuted or prohibited. And after the war, consider on the one hand the censorship that compromised if not actually stifled creativity in the Eastern Bloc under Soviet occupation, and on the other, score-settling within artistic circles that had collaborated with Fascist regimes or their puppet governments in Western Europe. Nevertheless it is true that after the war the Paris of Picasso, Giacometti and Dubuffet was still seen as the artistic Mecca for British artists to visit for at least the first post-war decade or so, during which time notably the British Council chose to fund its one and only permanent overseas arts officer in that city.

In Britain, however, a different situation had obtained throughout those war years and in its immediate aftermath. The Pilgrim Trust's launch of CEMA in 1940 and support given to Official War Artists was, ironically, not unlike the priority and protection given to cultural activity – within of course strict racial and stylistic boundaries on pain of persecution - in Nazi Germany during the war. But while Germany defeated and divided up among the Four Powers lay prostrate, Britain proceeded with the establishment of the Arts Council in 1945, enhanced by the 'soft power' of the British Council, the quasi-private initiative in 1947 of the cutting-edge interdisciplinary programmes of the I.C.A. and the arrival of Bryan Robertson at the Whitechapel Art Gallery in 1952. These initiatives and the expansion of the tertiary education sector (and the creation of the Welfare State) under the first post-war government, would combine to contribute to the effort needed, and the assistance given, to produce the Festival of Britain in 1951.

Hitler and Goebbels had also sponsored *their* Official War Artists, whose works glorifying battle were exhibited during the war, but obviously these works do not belong in the same category as the elegiac contemplation of destruction and suffering recorded by Moore, Nash, Piper, Sutherland and others, whose works were exhibited and admired at home during the war, and also abroad after it. Those Nazi war pictures remain locked up in Washington D.C. However, it should be said that Kenneth Clark's enlightened initiative in 1940 of 'Recording Britain' by commissioning British artists to paint in watercolours or draw scenes of the country's natural beauty, architectural heritage and way of life appears tame in comparison with the vast photographic record of Germany's built heritage, commissioned by the Nazi government as the war progressed. This would fortunately enable [West] Germany to rebuild so many of those churches, castles and palaces that were damaged or obliterated in the Allies' bombing campaigns.

It is sad to compare the extent of Germany's post-war restoration of its built heritage with the litany of accidental or deliberate loss recorded, for example, by Roy Strong in his exhibition 'The Destruction of the Country House' at the V & A in 1974. But then Germany had a task on hand: that of delivering proof of its 'de-Nazification' so as to qualify to rejoin the western democracies. One of the most effective ways to achieve this among opinion-formers would be to embrace and vigorously promote once again the modern theatre, music and art that the Nazis had prohibited. This Germany did with a vengeance, surpassing all the other western democracies in the restoration of the Weimar Republic's spread of progressive theatres, opera houses and art galleries across the capitals of its ten federal states. It would not be surprising if one found that, thanks in part to collaboration with the British Council and with some of the commercial galleries in London, by the 1960's one might have seen as much British contemporary painting and sculpture in those German state capitals' art galleries as in our own four National Galleries of modern art.

Philip Wright is a writer on some 20th century artists, galleries and collectors.

Sources and further reading

James Beechey & Chris Stephens (eds.), *Picasso & Modern British Art, Tate Britain & Scottish National Gallery of Modern Art, 2012*

Michael Bird, Lynn Chadwick, Lund Humphries, 2014

Alan Bowness, Bernard Meadows, Sculpture and Drawings, Henry Moore Foundation & Lund Humphries, 1995

Peter Black, Geoffrey Clarke, Symbols for Man, Sculpture and Graphic Work 1949-94, Ipswich Borough Council Museums & Galleries & Lund Humphries, 1994

David Brown, Corsham, a celebration: Bath Academy of Art 1946-72, Michael Parkin Gallery, 1989

Judith Collins, Eduardo Paolozzi, Lund Humphries & The Paolozzi Foundation, 2014

Penelope Curtis and others (eds.), Sculpture in 20th Century Britain, 2 vols., Henry Moore Institute, 2003

Penelope Curtis & Chris Stephens (eds.), Barbara Hepworth, Sculpture for a Modern World, Tate Publishing, 2015

Warren Forma, 5 British Sculptors (work and talk), Grossman Publishers, 1964

Margaret Garlake, New Art New World, British Art in Postwar Society, Yale University Press, 1998

Margaret Garlake, The Sculpture of Reg Butler, Henry Moore Foundation & Lund Humphries, 2006

A Silver Jubilee Exhibition of Contemporary British Sculpture, GLC/Battersea Park, 1977

Alastair Grieve, Constructed Abstract Art in England: a neglected avant-garde, Yale University Press, 2005

Alastair Grieve, The Sculpture of Robert Adams, Henry Moore Foundation & Lund Humphries, 1992

Martin Harrison, Transition, the London Art Scene in the Fifties, Merrell & Barbican Art Gallery, 2002

Jennifer Hawkins & Marianne Hollis (eds.), Thirties, British Art and Design before the War, Arts Council of Great Britain and Victoria & Albert Museum, 1979

Sandy Nairne & Nicholas Serota (eds.), British Sculpture in the Twentieth Century, Whitechapel Art Gallery, 1981

Benedict Read & David Thistlewood (eds.), Herbert Read, a British Vision of World Art, Leeds City Art Gallery, Henry Moore Foundation & Lund Humphries, 1993

Herbert Read, The Art of Sculpture (the 1954 Mellon Lectures), Faber & Faber, 1965

David Sylvester, Henry Moore, Arts Council of Great Britain & Tate Gallery, 1968

Illustrated Catalogue of Acquisitions, 7 vols., Tate Gallery, 1974-1988

Lisa Tickner & David Peters (eds.), British Art in the Cultural Field 1939-69, Wiley – Blackwell, 2012

Jane Turner (ed.), The Dictionary of Art, Macmillan, 1996

Germain Viatte & Henri-Claude Cousseau, Aftermath: France 1945-54, New Images of Man, Barbican Art Gallery, 1982

Alan Wilkinson (ed.), Henry Moore, Writings and Conversations, University of California Press, c2002

Simon Wilson, Picasso: Sculptor/Painter; a brief guide, Tate Gallery, 1994

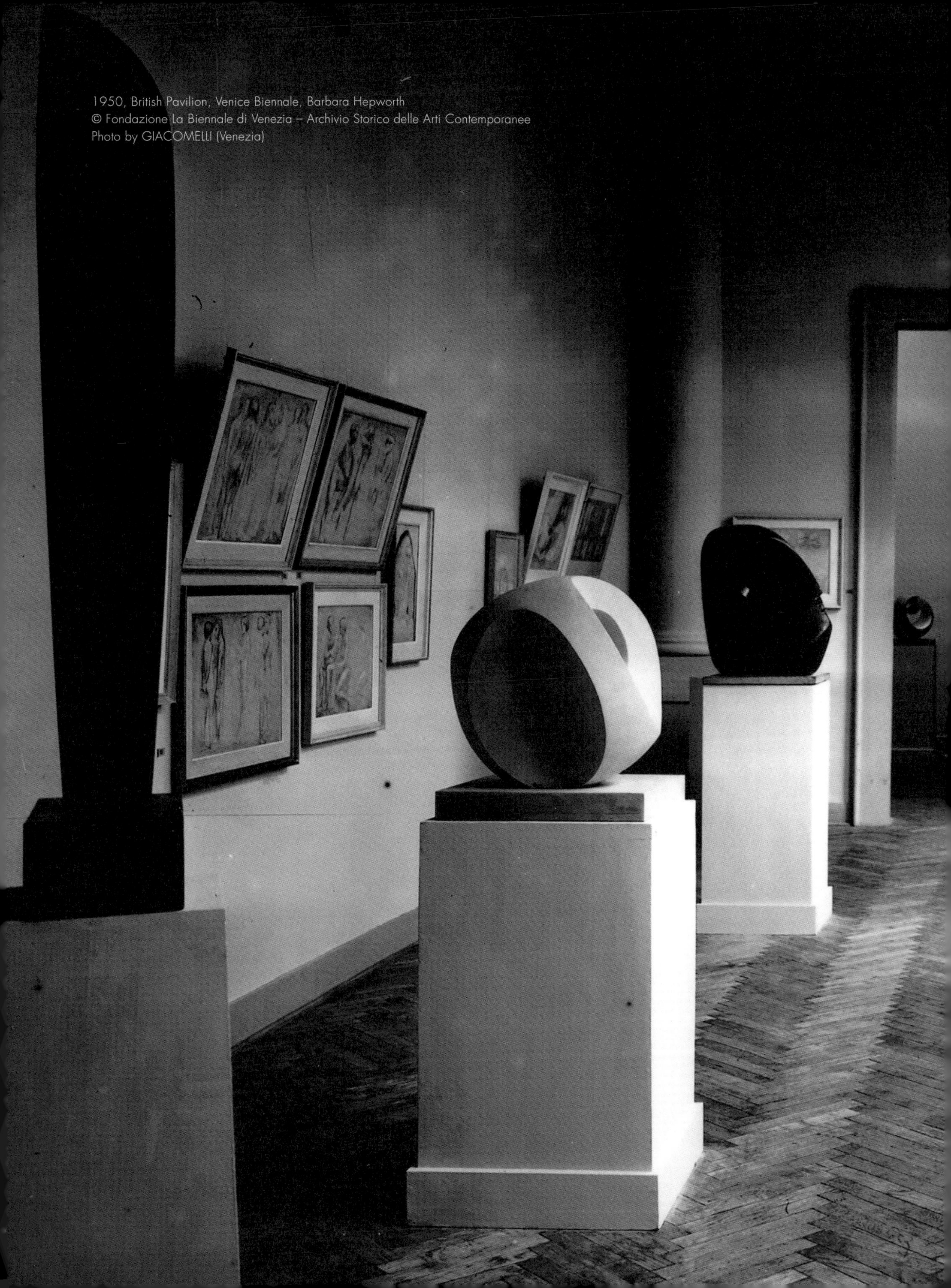

1950, British Pavilion, Venice Biennale, Barbara Hepworth

Photo by GIACOMELLI (Venezia)